P9-DOH-193

WHAT'S COOKING

down in

MAINE

by

Willan C. Roux

Cover and illustrations by Warren Spaulding

Down
East
BOOKS

Down East Books/*Camden, Maine*

For TRUDY . . .
Who proves daily that
The Best Wives Are Cooks
And Vice Versa

ACKNOWLEDGMENTS

To all of my friends on the islands as well as those in other parts of the state and the country whose constructive suggestions, criticism, and Maine interest have helped so much in preparing and writing this book.

To *Down East Magazine* in whose pages " The Ubiquitous Maine Lobster " and " The Maine Mollusks " first appeared.

To *The Brunswick Record,* particularly John Cole and Jane Lamb, for their early cooperation and encouragement, and for several recipes herein.

To *Maine-ly Recipes* by the Harpswell P.T.A., a source of much material.

To Mr. L. L. Bean for permission to feature him and to include some of his game and camp recipes.

To the Estate of Kenneth Roberts for permitting me to use three of his recipes that were published in *Trending into Maine,* copyright 1938 by Kenneth Roberts and N. C. Wyeth. Reprinted by permission of Doubleday & Company, Inc.

To the Estate of Robert P. Tristram Coffin and his daughter, Mrs. William E. Halvosa, for permission to reprint excerpts from the book *Mainstays of Maine,* published in 1944 by The Macmillan Company.

To Mr. Phineas Beck from whose *Clementine in the Kitchen* came Moules à la Mariniere, and to Mr. Marvin Small in whose book, *The World's Best Recipes,* I found it.

To Mr. Everett Greaton of the Maine Department of Economic Development and to the Maine Department of Sea and Shore Fisheries for assistance in gathering material.

To Mrs. James E. Coffin of Freeport for giving me the recipe for Poquahaug Chowder, a *chef d'ouevre* of her late husband, former Maine State Senator.

viii

TABLE OF CONTENTS

BY WAY OF INTRODUCTION

Probably the most significant ingredient in Down East cookery is common sense, a quality not necessarily exclusive to Maine, but nevertheless, an inborn characteristic of the people. Exotic seasonings and fancy trimmings have little place in their eatables. Yet imagination, originality, and distinction are in all of the dishes that come out of their kitchens.

Where but in Maine are lobster and fish so well understood and so well treated in the pot, the oven, and the skillet? Where else are there chowders and stews so simple in content yet such masterpieces of taste and consistency? Where is there more honest cooking, the kind that develops, without artifice, the nature-given flavor of every food?

To be sure, the products of Maine's shores and salt water are justly famous and their preparation and serving reasonably well known. But what of meat and potatoes, poultry, game, vegetables, bread, and cakes and pies? What about sauces and gravies, condiments, jellies and jams, native desserts? Here you will find culinary gems of equal note. Here is robust food as well as flavor-full dishes that rank, in gastronomic appeal, with much of the best cooking in America. A Maine boiled dinner, like a Maine clam chowder, is an unforgettable experience in good eating. And once you have tasted a Maine blueberry pie, you will never be satisfied with anything less!

It is about twenty years since the late Robert P. Tristram Coffin, Maine's "poet laureate," wrote "Mainstays of Maine," a series of essays in which the whole substance of Maine is woven into the substance of her foods. Essays, did I say? They are sheer poetry, singing the bounty of Maine's fields and waters, the hardiness and heartiness of her people, as well as the magic that they perform at the stove.

No book can pretend to be a Maine cookbook if it does not include a masterpiece or two from the Coffin menus: Father's chicken and dumplings, Mother's fall smelts, and Ruth Coffin's Indian pudding.

Nor can one ignore Kenneth Roberts, in whose "Trending into Maine" are several recipes that must have a place in "What's Cooking Down in Maine": bean-pot beans, homemade ketchup, and chocolate custard.

These are all of a piece with the others in this book—good, sound cooking that through the years has built strong men and capable, good-looking women—and continues to do so.

Many of the recipes that appear here are generations old, handed down, as so many recipes are, from mother to daughter, in farmhouses, fishing villages, and towns. Others are comparatively modern. Still others are favorite cooking formulas of my friends, my family, and myself.

Here, then, is "What's Cooking Down in Maine," a compendium modestly offered, not as an all-inclusive cookbook, but as a practical sampler of good Maine food.

WILLAN C. ROUX

Orr's Island, Maine
May, 1964

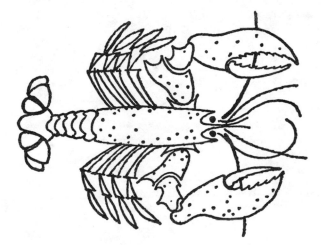

The lobster Down East is ubiquitous.
Though its appearance is highly iniquitous
Its meat and its juices
Have very fine uses:
And the flavor's sublime not ridiquitous!

I
FIRST THINGS FIRST:
THE UBIQUITOUS MAINE LOBSTER

What is there to add to the lore of the Maine lobster? No one, it is true, has written an ode to it or a dissertation to immortalize it, as Charles Lamb immortalized roast pig. Yet it merits such paeans, for surely it is the recognized monarch of the crustaceans.

National, if not international, in reputation, the Maine lobster travels to every corner of the United States. Its place on restaurant menus is as well established as coffee and tea. It is, without question, the lobster to which all others are compared. How often one hears "This is almost as good as a Maine lobster but . . . " There's always a "but," because there just isn't any lobster as good as that from Maine waters!

Thus it deserves to be coddled and prepared for the table with profound respect for its exclusive flavor, its firm meat, its luscious juices. And here in Maine it is treated with that respect and becomes, even in its simplest guises, a regal food, a truly epicurean delight!

Do You Boil It or Steam It?

As far as I am concerned, "you takes your choice." Either method is satisfactory, although I feel that steaming is preferable: there's not as much water to drain out of the lobster when it comes out of the pot, and the meat texture seems firmer yet more tender.

For boiling you need enough water (sea water if possible, otherwise well-salted fresh water) for complete immersion. The water should be boiling briskly when you dunk the lobsters headfirst. When the water comes back to a boil let them cook

3

for about 15 minutes. Take them out and put them on their backs to drain. Then serve them hot, with lots of melted butter.

For steaming you need only an inch of water in the pot, and when you have a good head of steam drop them in and give them about 18 minutes of cooking. (A nice touch: put in ½ cup of sherry. The flavor and sweetness of the meat will be enhanced considerably.)

Simple, isn't it? And in my opinion, about as fine a way as there is to enjoy the full, true flavor and succulent meat of a Maine lobster.

Steamed in Seaweed over Charcoal

We were introduced to this way of cooking lobster quite inadvertently and on full stomachs. We had just finished a rather sizable steak and were relaxing on the terrace, when along came Bill Boyce with a bucket of lobsters. (Bill, at that time, had a string of traps just off our dock and kept his punt there, so it was not unusual for him to bring us a few once in a while.)

After the customary greetings, Bill said: " I see there's some fire left. Ever eat a lobster cooked in seaweed over an open fire?" We all allowed we hadn't and protested that we had just eaten a big steak. "Never you mind," he went on, "lobster's good any time and I think I'll cook up a few for you to try."

While he gathered seaweed on the shore we groaned at the thought of lobster on top of steak. But there was no denying Bill.

So cook them he did. First he covered the top of the grill with a thick layer of seaweed, then nestled a half-dozen lobsters in it and covered them with another layer of weed. Soon the steam began to rise and the smell of cooking lobster filled the air. What it did to our taste buds was amazing: we actually developed a desire and an appetite! And when they were done we made short work of eating them (with Bill's help). Never have I tasted better. Oh yes, that night we passed up dessert!

Broiled, Indoors or Out

A broiled lobster is something special. It takes a little more doing than boiling or steaming, but the results are mighty satisfying.

Take a 2-pound live lobster and prepare to split it from head to tail. Be sure you hold the claws firmly with your left hand. W⁺th a sharp pointed knife make a deep incision at the mouth and draw the knife quickly through the entire length of the body and tail. Lay it out flat and remove the intestinal vein and stomach. Leave in the fat and liver (tomalley). Crack the claws.

Make a dressing of 1½ cups of crumbled common crackers moistened with 2 tablespoons of Worcestershire sauce and 4 tablespoons of butter. (That's enough for 4 lobsters, so add or subtract if you're cooking more or less.) Stuff the cavities full, cut off 4 small claws, and press them into the dressing. Broil 8 to 10 minutes on the flesh side, turn over, and broil 6 to 8 minutes on the shell side. Serve with melted butter.

Of course, if you don't want to bother with a dressing, just broil, dotting here and there with butter.

Over a Charcoal Grill

Make the same preparations as above (no dressing). Broil the shell side first and then the flesh side. Keep them moistened with butter. And don't be in a hurry. It'll take longer than it does in an oven broiler, but you'll know when they are ready and the wait will prove eminently worth while, particularly if you have a drink handy.

On an Engine's Exhaust Pipe

This may sound pretty silly to you, but if you ever have a chance to do it, don't miss it. It happened this way: Carl Skillings and I were codfishing one fine fall morning, near Half Way

Rock, and doing all right until the dogfish found us. It was getting on toward noon anyway and we were hungry. We hailed a friend of Carl's who was hauling traps near-by and borrowed a couple of lobsters from him. In no time the tails were split, the claws removed and cracked, and they were laid end to end on the exposed exhaust pipe. (We discarded the bodies.)

Soon we were eating them with cold beer as a chaser. Food for the gods? Well, maybe not, but at the time it seemed so!

Baked Stuffed Lobster

> *" 'Tis the voice of the lobster: I heard him declare,*
> *'You've baked me too brown ......'"*
> — *Alice in Wonderland*

If broiled lobster is something special, baked stuffed is something equally special. Heaven forbid that you bake him too brown!

Prepare the lobster as for broiling (split it, etc.). Make a dressing, using the fat, tomalley, rolled cracker crumbs, melted butter, and Worcestershire sauce. Stuff the cavities full, lay them on their backs in a shallow roasting pan, and put them in a 350 degree oven for about 40 minutes. Serve with melted butter.

Or you might prefer this more elaborate dressing: for four 2-pound lobsters, roll 16 common crackers into fine crumbs, mix in ¼ cup of melted butter and ¼ cup of milk. Then moisten to proper consistency with sherry. (You be the judge.) Finally, stir in 1 to 2 pounds of fresh crab meat, and stuff the lobsters as full as possible. Cook them as above and get ready for the finest kind of eating.

Serves 4

Maine Nectar: the Lobster Stew

The making of a proper lobster stew permits of no tri-fling. Simple as its ingredients are, they must be put together in an orderly manner and allowed to blend leisurely. Stirring and time are most important, the former to prevent curdling, the latter to "age" and thus develop the flavor to its fullest blossom. The following is the generally accepted method.

First boil or steam the lobster (a 2-pounder or 2 smaller ones), remove the meat immediately, cutting it into medium-sized pieces. Save the fat, the tomalley, and the coral (if any). Using a heavy kettle, simmer the tomalley, etc., in ½ cup of butter for 7 or 8 minutes. Put in the chunks of lobster and cook for 10 minutes more over low heat. Remove from heat and let it cool a bit. Then add, over low heat, very slowly, 1 quart of milk, stirring constantly. As soon as all the milk is in, remove from heat.

Now comes the aging: no matter how much you are tempted, let the stew stand 5 to 6 hours before reheating for serving. When you reheat, don't let it boil. Actually, the masters recommend 2 days for aging!

Note: Robert P. Tristram Coffin always added a cup or so of clam juice. Claimed it brought out the flavor.

Serves 4

Our Own Version

It's a bit fancier but you might like to try it sometime.

All you do that's different is to simmer the tomalley, etc., and lobster meat in ½ cup of butter and an equal amount of sherry. A few dashes of Worcestershire sauce and some paprika give it a good zip. Use half milk and half light cream. Follow the same procedure for stirring and aging. I've found that if you put the sherry in at the start, it permeates the stew but doesn't dominate it.

8 LOBSTERS

Then There's Captain Will Sylvester's Stew

Some years ago there was a bit of a dilemma on Orr's Island. Prominent people from upstate were coming to visit and speak at a town gathering. The day before, it was learned that they would arrive about suppertime and the women began to fidget because they hadn't planned much in the way of food.

Captain Will, however, took it all in stride. "We'll make 'em a lobster stew," he said.

Getting enough lobsters was no problem, and there was plenty of milk as well as butter on the island. Captain Will got the biggest washboiler he could find, filled it with sea water, and brought it to a brisk boil. Then he began putting lobsters in. He left them in only 4 or 5 minutes—just long enough to loosen the meat and not enough to cook it much. He set several women to work taking out the meat, making sure they saved all the juices, fat, and tomalley. Finally, after the cooling-off period, he put the meat back into the boiler on low heat and added the milk, stirring constantly as it flowed slowly into the pot. And that was that until the next day when he reheated it for serving to the VIP's and the home folks.

Anyone who was at that supper will tell you that they have never tasted a lobster stew to compare with it. The secret? Let Captain Will tell you.

"Never boil the lobster till it's all cooked, just enough so's the meat comes out easy and the juices flow free. That's all there is to it."

Well, I've done it this way—not in a washboiler but in moderate quantities—and it IS wonderful. All you need to do is to use the materials in proportion to the amount you want. (See the first recipe for stew, page 7.)

Pearl House Lobster Newburg

I doubt that Harriet Beecher Stowe ever had a lobster newburg like this when she was spending a summer in what is now our home on Orr's Island. However, this is the way we make it, and I think Harriet would have liked it too.

2 cups lobster meat in medium-sized pieces	1 cup light cream
2 tablespoons sherry	2 egg yolks, beaten
4 tablespoons butter	1 tablespoon lemon juice
1 tablespoon flour	Salt
	Paprika

Heat the lobster thoroughly in 3 tablespoons of the butter and the 2 tablespoons of sherry. Be careful not to brown the butter. In another saucepan, blend the rest of the butter with the flour, add the cream, and stir continually until the sauce boils. Remove from heat. Stir in the beaten egg yolks and return to the heat, stirring about 2 minutes until thickened. Add the heated lobster, lemon juice, and seasonings, and mix well but do not heat again. Serve immediately on toast points. Garnish with chopped water cress if you have any handy.

Serves 4

Mildred Hillman's Lobster Hash

Here is a homely dish that has a real quality of greatness.

Boil 2 lobsters 4 or 5 minutes as in Captain Will's stew—just enough to loosen the meat. Remove it from the shells and cut it into small pieces. Do not use the juice, tomalley, or fat—only the meat from the tail and claws.

Dice about ¼ pound of salt pork and try it out in a heavy skillet. You should have better than a couple of tablespoons of fat. Slice thinly a batch of raw potatoes, about one and a half times as much as the lobster. Start the potatoes frying in the fat. Add half a medium-sized onion, chopped, then the lobster. Keep chopping the mixture while it's cooking. (Mildred uses a tin can with both ends out, claiming this does the best job of chopping and stirring.) Cook until the potatoes are done, season to taste, and serve.

There'll be enough for 4 people—maybe!

Fried Lobster

A great favorite in our part of Maine. Use cooked lobster meat—you'll know how much you want. Melt butter in the skillet, put in the lobster, and add a generous dash of vinegar. Fry it until the meat is a bit browned.

Back Cove Lobster Glop

How this got its name no one seems to know. But after all, what's in a name? For by any name this is a fine dish and very easy to put together.

Crush enough common crackers to make 2 cups. Remove the meat from 2 boiled or steamed lobsters. Cut into medium-sized pieces. Melt ¼ pound of butter in the frying pan. Cook the lobster slightly. Add the cracker crumbs and enough milk to make it "sloppy." Keep stirring until it thickens. Salt and pepper to taste. Serve with Maine baked potatoes. This will stick to your ribs.

Makes 2-4 servings

The Bailey Island Lobster Bake

This is a real production but reasonably easy to manage, whether it's for a half-dozen eager eaters or a hundred, according to Ken Oliver and Bill Skillings, who are the perennial bake masters. The only rule is to have enough of everything: seconds are usual and thirds quite frequent at this lobster bake.

It all starts with a metal barrel or drum (55 gallon) which has been cut in half lengthwise. Place it across rocks, leaving at least a foot underneath for space to build a fire. Just barely cover the bottom of the drum with sea water, then put in a layer of seaweed. Steamer clams go in first. Put a dozen clams with a little water in each of as many plastic bags as you will need. Cover them with more seaweed and a piece of burlap soaked in water. Then another layer of seaweed in which you place the lobsters. More seaweed and a wet piece of burlap. Again seaweed and now sweet corn in the husks. Repeat seaweed and burlap and you're ready for the final layer—sweet potatoes and eggs. Finally cover the half-drum with a piece of wet canvas.

Light the fire and sit back to enjoy a drink or two. Keep the fire well stoked and the canvas wet, and in an hour everything's ready.

Have lots of melted butter ready and go to it with your hands—clams first, then all the rest. You may need a bath afterward, but that's a small price to pay for a very great eating experience.

Maine Lobster Bake—Barbecue Style

An easy and very satisfactory way to have a bake on your charcoal grill. When it's done each person will have an individual " package " ready to eat. This one is figured for six servings.

6 dozen Maine steamer clams	6 live Maine lobsters (1¼
6 medium Maine baking	pounds each)
potatoes	Rockweed (optional)
6 medium onions	Lemon wedges
6 ears of corn, in the husks	Melted butter

Wash clam shells thoroughly. Wash potatoes and cut off ends. Peel onions. Remove corn silk from ears of corn and replace husks. Cut 12 pieces of cheesecloth and 12 pieces of heavy-duty aluminum foil, 18 x 36 inches each. Place 2 pieces of cheesecloth on top of 2 sheets of foil. Place 12 clams, a lobster, potato, onion, ear of corn, and some rockweed on cheesecloth. Tie the cheesecloth up over the food. Pour 1 cup of water over the package. Bring edges of the foil together and seal tightly. Make 6 of these packages. Place them on a barbecue grill about 4 inches from hot coals. Cover with hood or aluminum foil. Cook for 1 hour, or until potatoes are cooked, turning every 15 minutes. Serve with lemon wedges and melted butter.

Thus, the Ubiquitous Maine Lobster

Even without dissertations or paeans of praise, it is certain that the Maine lobster can stand on his own little claws, his reputation sure, his place high in the culinary world. For no matter how you prepare him or serve him, he is always a gustatory marvel and a joy forever.

I do not pretend that the foregoing methods of cooking are the last word or the only ways of enjoying lobster, but they are ways that are tried and true hereabouts; and that's good enough for me.

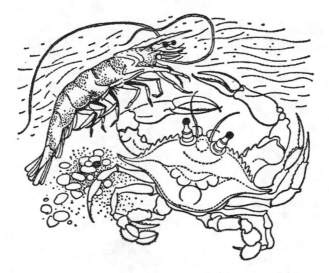

The crab and the shrimp are crustaceans.
Though lower than lobster their stations,
In Maine they are sought
And quite generally bought
To become the most happy collations.

II
LESSER MAINE CRUSTACEANS:
THE CRAB AND THE SHRIMP

THE CRAB

For the most part, Maine crabs are caught in lobster traps: a sort of by-product of the lobstering business. Years ago any lobsterman would give you a bucketful for the asking. Later they sold for a penny apiece. (In those days, lobster could be bought for 10 to 15 cents a pound.) Today, fresh Maine crab meat is available in half-pound and pound packages, in stores as well as from housewives along the coast.

It is unfortunate that it is not widely available outside the state. But if you can't make it Down East every time you want a crab dish, you'll find you can use these sound recipes with any other crab meat and enjoy the results almost as much.

My Mother's Deviled Crab

It must be about fifty years since I first tasted this deviled crab. That was when crabs were for free and Will Merriman brought us a mess of them anytime Mother asked him. When they were cooked and cooling on the porch, my sister and I would snap off a claw or two and duck fast. Mother always demurred, if she caught us, because she was afraid there wouldn't be enough. Somehow there always was—and to spare. Here's her recipe:

1 cup milk	4 yolks hard-boiled eggs,
2 tablespoons flour	mashed
1 tablespoon butter	1 tablespoon minced parsley
1 pint crab meat or	Salt and cayenne to taste
12 boiled crabs	Beaten egg
1 tablespoon chopped onion	Bread crumbs

15

Combine the butter, flour, and milk to make a cream sauce. Stir in the crab meat, onion, mashed egg yolks, and parsley, and season to taste. Fill the shells (or ramekins if you don't have empty crab shells). Brush with beaten egg and cover with bread crumbs. Brown in a quick oven.

Mother never bothered with exact oven heat or the time it took to cook things. When they were done, they were done—and she knew it. And with this dish, so will you.

Serves 4

Southern Maine Crab Soup

Charleston, South Carolina, She-crab Soup is a gourmet's delight, deserving every bit of acclaim that comes its way. Without detracting from its reputation, I submit a Southern Maine (Casco Bay) crab soup that favors neither gender of crab but develops into a delight of equal merit.

6 common crackers	1 quart milk
2 tablespoons butter	Salt and pepper
2 cups fresh crab meat	1 can evaporated milk
½ cup water	(13 oz.)

Pulverize the crackers to make them as fine as flour. Melt butter in kettle and put in the crumbs and crab meat. Add the water and let it bubble for one minute, no more. This, for some reason or other, brings out the full, luscious flavor of the crab. Pour in the fresh milk and stir continually until small bubbles show on the surface. Do not let it boil now or later. Season to taste with salt and pepper. Add the evaporated milk, keep stirring, and bring it just to the boiling point. Serve with heated common crackers.

Two things you can do, if you want: 1) Cook it in a double boiler to eliminate constant stirring, and 2) add a couple of tablespoons of sherry before serving.

Makes 5-6 servings

Boothbay Harbor Crab Cakes

This was featured, circa 1945, in "The State of Maine's Best Seafood Recipes" and it has lost none of its appeal and zest over the years. Served with a lobster sauce, it is a worthy pièce de résistance at any meal. A crisp green salad is a perfect complement.

3 eggs, separated	1 teaspoon minced green
1½ cups crab meat	pepper
1 cup crumbled common	1 teaspoon minced celery
crackers	1/3 teaspoon salt
¼ cup melted butter	1/8 teaspoon pepper
2 teaspoons lemon juice	

Beat the egg yolks. Mix in the crab meat, cracker crumbs, melted butter, and all the other ingredients. Blend them well. Stiffly beat the egg whites, fold them into the mixture, and turn into four well-greased custard cups or molds. Set them in a pan of hot water and bake in a 375 degree oven for 25 minutes. Unmold and serve with this lobster sauce:

LOBSTER SAUCE

To 1 cup hot medium white sauce add ½ cup of finely flaked cooked lobster. Heat well and pour over the crab cakes.

Makes 4 servings

Island Crab Cakes

Our local crab cakes, like fish cakes, are simple to prepare and just plain good to eat.

2 eggs	2/3 cup broken common
1 small onion, minced	crackers
1 pound fresh crab meat	1 teaspoon salt
1 tablespoon mayonnaise	1/8 teaspoon pepper

Beat eggs slightly with fork, add onion. Put in crab meat, mayonnaise, crackers, salt and pepper and shape into cakes. Sauté in a little fat.

Makes 4-6 servings

Crab Meat Au Gratin

An easy and very satisfactory way of serving crab. Personally I'm a pushover for things au gratin.

1 cup milk	½ teaspoon salt
1 tablespoon flour	2 cups fresh crab meat
2 tablespoons butter	Enough sliced American cheese
1 teaspoon Worcestershire	to cover
sauce	Paprika

Combine first five ingredients to make a white sauce. Add the crab meat. Put into a greased baking dish and top it with slices of cheese. Sprinkle with paprika. Bake at 350 degrees until cheese melts (about 20 minutes).

Makes 4 servings

Crab Meat Stuffing

This is a mixture I'm sure you'll find to your taste in baked green peppers or tomatoes, or as a dressing for poultry, lobster, or fish.

1 cup crab meat	¾ cup chopped celery
2 eggs, slightly beaten	2 slices bacon, uncooked
2 tablespoons butter	1 cup fresh bread crumbs
1 medium onion, chopped	Salt and pepper

Flake the crab meat and add the eggs. Fry in butter the chopped onion, celery, bacon (cut into small pieces), and bread crumbs. Cook over low heat until the ingredients are tender. Add the crab-meat mixture, and season to taste.

Will stuff 6 peppers

THE SHRIMP

Shrimp, fortunately, do not paddle around just in the waters of the deep south. They have found Maine and other waters above the Mason-Dixon line much to their liking and thus to ours. The only thing is, I'm sorry to say, there aren't as many of them up this way. And they don't grow up to become even small prawns. But for their size (about 3 inches from head to tail), they are delicious morsels, very special and very delicate in flavor. They are truly equal in character to any I have ever tasted, including those caught in the creeks and inlets of the Carolina Low Country and sold by the Negro hucksters who cry their wares in the streets: "Swimpee, raw. Raw swimp!" Maine shrimp or Carolina swimp—they're great.

Here the fishermen drag for them with nets during an all too short three-month season and sell them by the pound or the bushel to local fishmongers, stores, and people like me. Right now I have a freezer full.

Boiling Shrimp

The primary rule with shrimp, as with most other sea foods, is "cook it short." It can be overcooked so easily that it is important to follow this simple procedure for best results:

Start with a small amount of cold water into which you have dropped some pickling spice for flavor. Put in the shrimp in their shells (remove the heads only). When the water comes to a boil, cook for not more than 5 minutes. Drain, run cold water through them and let cool. De-shell and de-vein them, and they're ready to eat or to use in any of the following recipes.

Shrimp Wiggle

The name has always intrigued me. Even though it is defined in the dictionary, I can't help wondering why and how it was so christened: "wiggle . . . a dish of creamed shellfish or fish with peas." Anyway, this is how it's done and it is good.

2 tablespoons butter	1 cup shrimp
2 tablespoons flour	½ medium onion (not sliced)
1½ cups warm milk	2/3 cup cooked peas
Salt and pepper	

Make a medium white sauce (it should not be too thick) by melting the butter over direct heat, adding the flour, cooking and stirring until smooth, then pouring the milk in gradually and stirring until slightly thickened. Remove to a double boiler, add the shrimp, the ½ onion, and the peas. Heat thoroughly (15 to 20 minutes). Take out the onion and season with salt and pepper to taste. Serve very hot over crisp crackers or toast.

Serves 4

Extra Twist with a Wiggle: add tomato soup and rice to make a hearty main dish:

Put 1 tablespoon of butter in the top part of your double boiler, then 1 tablespoon of chopped onion, 1 cup of boiled rice, ½ can of tomato soup, a dash of red pepper, and a little salt. Cook until the onion is done. Now add 1 cup of cream, 2 cups of cooked shrimp, 2 cups of peas, and reheat thoroughly: do not boil. Serve on crackers, toast, or in patty shells.

Serves 6

Shrimp Newburg

Follow the recipe for Lobster Newburg on page 9, using 2 cups of cooked shrimp.

Shrimp Chowder

This is not, in my opinion, a true chowder, but that's what it's called here and I see no reason to argue. Nor will you when you taste it.

¼ cup chopped onion	Cayenne
¼ cup diced salt pork	4 cups hot milk
2 tablespoons butter	2 cups shrimp
2 tablespoons flour	1 cup hot cream
Salt	(or evaporated milk)

Cook the onion in the salt pork until golden (not brown). In another pan melt the butter, put in the flour and seasonings, blending well. Add the hot milk, stirring until smooth and slightly thickened. Place in the top part of your double boiler, add the shrimp, and cook over low heat for 20 minutes. Strain the salt pork fat and add. Then add the hot cream. Reheat without boiling.

Serves 4

Note: I've found that shrimp instead of crab meat in the Southern Maine Crab soup on page 16 is a delicious switch. The shrimp should be cut into small pieces.

Shrimp Puffs

These are deep fried, and like peanuts, they always taste like more!

2 cups flour	1 egg
½ teaspoon salt	1 cup milk
3 teaspoons baking powder	½ pound shrimp

Sift the dry ingredients—flour, salt, and baking powder. Beat the egg and add it to the milk and shrimp, then stir this into the flour mixture and mix it thoroughly. Drop from a large spoon into a kettle of hot fat and fry to a delicate brown.

Either lobster or crab can be done this way with equally satisfying results.

Makes 4-6 servings

Fried Shrimp

Make a batter of ½ cup of flour, ¼ teaspoon of salt, 1 egg, and 1/3 cup of milk. Sprinkle the shrimp (as many as you think you will need) with lemon juice (this develops a fine flavor). Dip the shrimp in the batter, fry until brown on one side, then turn and brown on the other.

22 THE SHRIMP

Other Ways with Crab and Shrimp

I'm sure I don't have to tell you that both crab and shrimp make excellent cocktails, are wonderful in salads, and that among other things, you can curry them, make casseroles, bake them, and broil them—in fact, their uses are limited only by your imagination.

I submit the above with due deference to other, perhaps more glamorous dishes, but without any apology for their very ample goodness and Down East constitution.

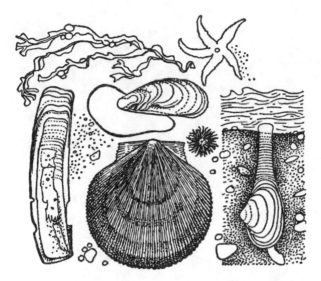

The mollusks are quite closely related
But have never as yet inter-mated.
They stick to their classes
Resisting all passes
And thus are not well integrated.

III

THE MAINE MOLLUSKS:
CLAMS, QUAHOGS, SCALLOPS, AND MUSSELS

Nostalgia raises its lovely head as I think back to my early summers in Maine (circa 1912): to milk poured out of pans in Clarendon Bibber's cold cellar—at five cents a quart; to wild strawberries and fields of blueberries; to our own vegetable garden, and to the seemingly inexhaustible clam beds on the shore in front of the cottage.

Living was simple and good, and a clam chowder was a whole meal. We were unaware of any pretenders to the clam chowder name and couldn't have cared less. But in the interim I have conscientiously, and sometimes vehemently, had to protect the virtue of Maine chowder from assaults by the Manhattan vegetable soup with clams and the thickened variety of so-called chowder that is found in certain other sections of the country. Let's have done with this controversy about what is and what is not a clam chowder!

The word chowder comes from the French word " chaudière," meaning kettle or pot. Webster is reasonably explicit in defining a chowder: " a dish made of fresh fish or clams, pork, crackers, onions, etc., stewed together, often in milk; by extension, a similar dish in which a vegetable, as corn, replaces the fish."

That seems direct enough. Instead of crackers use potatoes, and if you follow the directions below you'll arrive at perfection with the true, uncomplicated, incomparable Maine clam chowder.

25

Maine Clam Chowder

I don't care whether you use freshly shucked soft clams or quahogs or both. Nor do I care if you use canned clams, as I have done many times. But if you attempt any deviation or variation in this basic way of making your chowder, I'll take no responsibility for the results. An authentic Maine clam chowder wants no fussing with, even if you have a mind to: you cannot improve on it!

¼ pound salt pork	1 quart Maine clams
1 quart diced potatoes	1 quart rich milk, scalded
1 large onion, chopped	Salt and pepper
1 tablespoon butter	

Dice the pork and fry in the chowder pot until brown. Add the potatoes and onion with just enough water to be seen through the potatoes. Cook over low heat—just simmering—until done. Strain clams and save the juice. Add the clams to the potatoes and onions and cook for 2 minutes after they come to a full boil. (Any longer will make the clams tough.)

Remove pot from heat and let it stand for a few minutes. Then add the hot milk and the clam juice, and season to taste. This way there's less chance of the chowder curdling. Add a tablespoon of butter just before serving.

For the best flavor, let it sit for a while—at least a few hours: aging is as important for a clam chowder as for a lobster stew. If you can wait until the next day it'll be that much finer. And, by the way, have a lot of heated common crackers ready.

Makes 6-8 servings

Clam Stew

Each portion calls for a dozen small, tender clams and 1½ cups of milk. Sauté the clams in a frying pan in their own juice, a little butter, and sal. and pepper to taste. Heat the milk in the top part of a double boiler.

Put the clams into individual heated serving bowls with a small piece of butter. Pour in the hot milk and serve immediately.

Simple, easily done, and distinctly worth the doing. Try it some night when the wind is out of the north and there's snow in the air.

Steamed Clams

It's hard to go wrong steaming clams and the sky's the limit on the number you can eat at one sitting. When we have them, a half peck does nicely for two people.

The smaller the clams the better they are for steaming. Place them in a large kettle with 2 cups of water. Cover and let them steam until the shells open. Serve them very hot with plenty of melted butter and mugs of the clam broth. I like to lace the broth with a little celery salt.

Fried Clams

In Maine they call these the "best ever fried clams" and you'll have no quarrel with that claim.

1 egg, separated	¼ teaspoon salt
½ cup milk	½ cup sifted flour
1 tablespoon melted butter	2 dozen clams (at least)

There's a bit of work in making them: here's how. Beat the egg yolk, add half the milk, and the butter. Mix the salt with the flour, sift it, and beat it into first mixture, stirring until smooth. Then add the remaining milk and fold in the egg white, stiffly beaten.

Drain the clams and dip each one into the batter, frying in deep fat (375 F.) until golden brown. Drain on absorbent paper. Ketchup is optional. Personally I like them plain and unadorned.

While this recipe is supposed to serve four or five, I'm of the opinion that 6 clams apiece just aren't enough. A dozen is more like it—so double the recipe if you agree.

Clams a la Prout

Here is a real jewel from a Mrs. Blatchley of Guilford, Connecticut. She sent it to the Maine Development Commission in 1945. Her letter tells it far better than I can:

When we were married in 1898 a Mr. Henry Prout (called by all Capt.) who was originally from Maine, a fisherman all his life, gave me this recipe which is delicious and as Down East as can be. I had it put in a church cookbook and named it Clams à la Prout.

Boil potatoes and cool, or use left over from dinner. Steam clams and pick them out, saving the broth. To prepare, slice some salt pork in hot frying pan, not too brown. Put in sliced boiled potatoes. Pour over clams (whole) and broth. Cook together, stirring occasionally until the broth is cooked down to make like creamed sauce, not very much. Put in dish and serve piping hot. This is delicious flavor and a Maine fisherman's own recipe.

Now the questions are: how many potatoes, how many clams, and how much salt pork? Captain Prout and Mrs. Blatchley undoubtedly knew, but I had to find out by trial and error reconstruction: use the same quantities as in a chowder and you've got it made.

Water Cove Baked Clams

Shuck medium to large clams, being sure not to break the shells. Clean the clams and wash the shells. Place each clam on a half shell and fill with your favorite stuffing (see Broiled or Baked Lobster if you need help). Put on the top shell and bake 1 hour. Serve while hot.

Clam Cakes

This recipe appeared in a local cookbook some years ago, a concoction devised by one Laura McClintock.

1 pint chopped clams   1½ cups cracker crumbs
2 eggs, unbeaten

Mix clams and crumbs together. Add eggs one at a time and mix well. Let sit a few moments to soften crumbs. Mixture should hold together but be moist. Fry in butter in skillet, dropping in large spoonfuls of mixture and pressing them down to make cakes ¾ inches thick. Fry on one side until brown, then turn and brown the other side. If common crackers are used, season with salt. Do not add salt if saltine crackers are used. The liquid from the clams may be used.

Today people call these cakes "clamburgers." Oh well!

Serves 4

Aunt Lesley's Clam Fritters

How good these used to taste when I was growing up! As a matter of fact, they still do. Time hasn't dimmed their appeal the way it has my appetite.

Beat the yolks of 2 eggs until they are thick and lemon-colored. Add ½ cup of milk, 1 teaspoon of cooking oil, 1 cup of sifted flour, ¼ teaspoon of salt, and 1 teaspoon of baking powder.

Fold in 2 stiffly beaten egg whites and put in 1 pint of chopped clams. Let this stand in the icebox for at least two hours.

Drop batter from spoon into deep hot fat and fry until golden brown. Fry only a few at a time so the fat won't cool down.

Will serve 4 or 5

Orr's Island Deep-Dish Clam Pie

Another of Mildred Hillman's fine dishes, this is a meal in itself, served with a crisp green salad. Line your deep dish with an unbaked pie shell. Put in a layer of raw clams. Sift flour over them, add salt and pepper. Repeat layers to fill dish, then top it with pie pastry. Bake in a moderate oven for 30 minutes.

4-6 servings

Clam Muddle

Used as a gravy over baked potatoes, this mixture is easy to make and very rewarding.

Fry diced salt pork until brown, add raw clams and a little water. Cook until clams are done, then add flour to thicken. That's it.

QUAHOGS

Of incidental interest: these hard-shelled clams, harvested in Maine primarily in our area, Casco Bay, are the most scientifically managed of any of the state's marine resources. Bless the management for its good work!

Small though the quahog yield is compared with soft-shell clams, they are, nonetheless, of exceptional quality, succulent and of fine flavor. They can be, and are, being used in all the ways that soft clams are, with equally delicious results. And they are wonderful served raw on the half shell—which you can't say for soft clams.

So use all the foregoing recipes with quahogs if you prefer them. Personally I do not like them steamed, but you may and that's all that counts.

There is, however, one unforgettable recipe that must be included here—a chowder that has not only charmed the palates of thousands but has also played a part in Maine's political life. I give you

Senator Coffin's Poquahaug Chowder

Poquahaug was the Indian name from which quahog is derived and the late James E. (Ned) Coffin of Freeport, Maine, thus named his chowder. A man whose looks and homespun philosophy were a reminder of the late Will Rogers, he wrote stories about Freeport history and Yankee trading under the name of "The Eel Skinner."

During his campaign for State Senator some years ago, he used the chowder as a conversation piece and a "jollifier" and maintained that "the hand that stirs the chowder, shows the way." In this case it certainly did, for he was the first Democrat elected to the State Senate from the Freeport area since 1914.

This "gem from the chowder bucket," as he called it, uses the following ingredients:

½ peck quahogs	1 cup clam bouillon
1 pint soft clams, shucked	1/3 spoon crushed red pepper
1 pound lobster	2 pinches oregano
2½ pounds potatoes	3 snakes garlic salt
1 small onion	Regular salt to taste
¼ pound butter	2 quarts milk
1/8 pound salt pork, diced	1 small can evaporated milk

Steam the quahogs, remove from shells, and chop. Also chop the soft clams. Boil the lobster and chop it—use everything but the shell—sauté in butter. Cut the potatoes into ⅝ inch cubes and boil them lightly. Chop and sauté the onion in butter. Fry the diced salt pork, throw away the fat, using only the fried pieces in the chowder.

Now to put it together: pour the bouillon into the chowder pot, add the quahogs, the clams, the lobster, the potatoes, the onion, the pork scraps, and the seasonings. Simmer until the potatoes are done, then add the milk and evaporated milk and heat but do not let it boil.

Finally, as Mr. Coffin said: "Always prepare chowder and let it cool without cover. Then heat it for ideal results."

Serves 6 amply

SCALLOPS

Maine scallops are tender morsels that lend themselves with distinction to various methods of cooking: frying, broiling, baking, stewing, creaming, and in salads. They reward you with a rich goodness that makes them a rare treat any way you fix them.

Fried Scallops

To serve four, use one pound (1 pint) of scallops. Pat them dry with paper toweling. If they are bigger than ¾ inch, cut them down to size. Roll in seasoned flour then in slightly beaten egg, diluted with milk or water (1 tablespoon for each egg). Then roll them again in seasoned flour mixed half and half with bread crumbs. Fry in deep fat (375 F) for about 4 minutes. It's best to put only a single layer in the greased frying basket so they will be evenly browned. Skim fat and reheat it if necessary before cooking another batch. Drain on soft paper. Serve with tartar sauce or ketchup.

Serves 4

Baked Scallops

Roll one pound of dried scallops in flour and put them in a greased pan. Fill to about half the depth of scallops with rich milk. Dot with butter; salt and pepper to taste. After they've baked about a half hour in a 350 degree oven, turn them over and brown the other side. A too-hot oven curdles the milk and makes it unsightly.

Serves 4

Sauteed Scallops

Have one pound of scallops at room temperature and dry. Dust lightly with flour and cook for 3 minutes in butter that is almost smoking hot. Turn them occasionally. Season on plate.

Serves 4

Broiled Scallops

This is our own way of doing them.

Dry one pound of scallops. Dip them in beaten egg and cracker crumbs. Arrange them in a large pan, dot each scallop with butter or bacon fat. Broil them or bake them until they are crisp and hot. Be sure not to cook them too long. Twenty minutes will do.

Serves 4

Broiled Scallops, Fancied Up

Though not really Down East cooking we've done it with Maine scallops, so that makes it all right with my conscience.

1½ pounds scallops	½ teaspoon minced garlic
½ cup dry Vermouth	½ teaspoon salt
½ cup olive oil	2 tablespoons minced parsley

Marinate the scallops in the Vermouth and other ingredients for several hours. Put scallops and marinade in shallow pan 2 inches from the heat of a pre-heated broiler. Cook 5 to 6 minutes.

Serves 4-6

Note: Cut them into smaller pieces and serve them as appetizers with cocktails. M-m-m!

Scallop Stew

Cut 1 pound of scallops into half-inch pieces and sauté them. gently in 3 tablespoons of butter for 15 minutes. Add one quart of milk, warmed slightly, salt and pepper to taste. Heat just to the boiling point and serve in heated bowls.

For a nice touch, sprinkle a bit of chopped parsley over each serving.

Serves 4

Scallop Casserole

Cut 1½ pints (or pounds) of scallops into ¾-inch cubes. Melt 4 tablespoons of butter in a saucepan and add half an onion, minced fine. Sauté until golden and tender. Stir in 4 tablespoons of flour with 1 teaspoon of salt and ¼ teaspoon of pepper. When well blended, slowly add 2 cups of warm milk. Blend and stir until thickened. Add ½ teaspoon of dry mustard, 1 tablespoon of lemon juice, and 2 tablespoons of minced parsley and chives. Cook and stir over low heat until smooth.

Add the cubed scallops and turn all into a greased baking dish. Sprinkle with buttered crumbs and paprika. Bake in a moderate oven (350 F) about 20 minutes, or until browned on top.

Serves 6

Scallop Salad

1 pint scallops	1 cup diced celery
1 quart boiling water	¼ cup chopped sweet pickle
1 tablespoon lemon juice	½ tablespoon salt
1 cup mayonnaise	Lettuce

Cook scallops 10 minutes in boiling water to which lemon juice and salt have been added. Drain well. Chill and cut into quarters (or more if the scallops are large). Add mayonnaise, celery, pickles, and mix lightly. Chill for 1 hour and serve on lettuce.

Serves 6

Scallop Cakes

1 pint scallops	2 teaspoons baking powder
2 eggs	Milk
2 cups flour	Salt and pepper

Cut scallops (if they are large) and parboil them. Drain and chop very fine. Beat eggs slightly and add flour sifted with baking powder. Mix with enough milk to make a batter to drop easily from a spoon. Beat well together and add scallops. Heat drippings in a spider, drop batter by spoonfuls into the hot grease. Sprinkle with seasonings. Brown, turn, and brown on other side.

Serves 4

MUSSELS

Mussels are possibly the most neglected and unappreciated sea food in America. But in Italy, France, and Maine they are neither neglected nor unappreciated: they are thoroughly enjoyed.

At their best in the early spring, Maine mussels are plump and tender. And the supply is unlimited. They are to be found along the entire length of the coast, clinging to the rocks and ledges in great clusters, blue-black beauties waiting to be picked when the tide is out. It's a pity that more of them don't reach other parts of the country. We'd like to share their goodness with you in any of the following ways:

Steamed Mussels

Be sure to scrub the mussels well with a wire brush or a steel scouring pad. Then place them in a large kettle with a half inch of water in the bottom. Cover and let them steam until the shells open. As with clams, serve them very hot with plenty of melted butter and mugs of the broth.

Or Steam them in Wine

Use dry white wine instead of the water. Throw in half a bay leaf and a small clove of garlic. You'll be glad you did! The mussels and broth take on a gustatory glow that the French have a word for: magnifique!

Mussel Stew

Follow the recipe for clam stew on page 26.

Mussel Soup

A hearty soup that finds considerable favor here. The ingredients:

6–8 dozen mussels	2 cups milk, scalded
3 cups mussel liquor	1 egg yolk
6 medium-size onions	1 tablespoon minced pimento,
3 tablespoons butter	if desired
4 tablespoons flour	

Steam the mussels until they open. Reserve 3 cups of the liquor. Remove the mussel meat from the shells—there should be about 1 quart of it. Chop the onions, sauté slowly in 2 tablespoons of the butter for about 5 minutes, or until golden and partly tender. Add mussel meat liquor, cover and cook for 30 minutes. Press the mixture through a sieve. Set aside. Melt the remaining butter in a saucepan. Make a paste of the flour by stirring it smooth in a little of the warm milk, using a separate bowl. Gradually add the rest of the milk, stirring to incorporate well. Add this mixture with the mussel meat and seasonings to the melted butter. Cook and stir steadily over low heat for 5 minutes.

Add the sieved mixture, then stir in the slightly beaten egg yolk, and add pimento, if desired. Reheat about 1 minute, not boiling.

Serves 6 to 8

Baked Mussels—an Old Favorite

Thoroughly scrub and wash in running cold water 5 dozen fresh mussels. Place them in a saucepan with 1 pint of water and 1 teaspoon of salt. Cover and let them steam for about 15 minutes. Remove, drain, take them out of the shells and remove the little hairy appendage found under the black tongue.

Put the mussels in a casserole, season with ½ teaspoon of salt and ½ teaspoon of paprika and sprinkle with ½ teaspoon of finely chopped parsley and ½ teaspoon of minced onion. Cover with 5 or 6 slices of salt pork and sprinkle 1 tablespoon of grated cheese over the top. Place in a moderately hot oven to bake 15 or 20 minutes, or until pork is crisp.

Serves 5

Fried Mussels

Allow at least 1 dozen mussels per person.

Wash mussels, drain and dry well—after you've shucked them, of course. Roll in flour that has been seasoned to taste with salt and pepper. Dip in slightly beaten egg diluted with 1 tablespoon of cold water. Roll in fine cracker or bread crumbs. Fry in shallow or deep hot fat (375 F) until golden brown. Drain on soft paper.

Scalloped Mussels

Scrub one quart of mussels, cover with hot water, and bring quickly to the boiling point. Drain. Remove from shells.

Combine about 2 cups of bread crumbs with 2 tablespoons of melted butter. Place a layer of buttered crumbs in a greased baking dish. Add a layer of mussels, sprinkle with minced green pepper (you may need 2 peppers for this), and season with salt and pepper.

Repeat until dish is full. Pour over enough rich milk to moisten, and sprinkle with buttered crumbs. Bake 30 minutes in a moderate oven (350 F).

Serves 6

A Touch of Europe for Maine Mussels

While my original intent for this culinary sampler was to confine it strictly to Down East dishes, I am so fond of mussels that I must include three recipes that are European but much to be desired. Mussels are so beautifully treated in Italy and France— and I wish the same for the Maine variety!

Moules a la Mariniere (Peasant Version)

Featured in "The World's Best Recipes," by Marvin Small, from the book "Clementine in the Kitchen," by Phineas Beck, this is a simple French recipe that deserves its high gourmet status.

2 quarts mussels	Minced parsley
4 or 5 sections garlic	Freshly ground pepper
2 ounces butter	

Brush and scrape the mussel shells, wash in several waters, clipping the "beard" with a knife. Place the mussels in a pan, add garlic, chopped fine, a good fistful of minced parsley, a little freshly ground pepper, and the butter. Salt is not needed.

Cover the pan, place over a brisk fire and cook for 5 or 6 minutes, shaking the pan 2 or 3 times. Remove the lid.

The mussels are open, ready to be served with their own sauce in soup plates.

Makes 3-4 servings

Mussels a la Rita

Friends of ours brought back from Italy a wonderful cook who, soon after her arrival, discovered mussels on the shore and went into ecstasies. She was used to buying them in the markets and her thrifty soul rejoiced at finding all she could ever use free for the gathering.

Her baked mussels, served to us as appetizers, were superlative. She made a stuffing of bread crumbs, minced onion, and finely chopped green pepper, moistened with dry red wine and seasoned to taste, including a touch of garlic. (The stuffing should be on the dry side.) She arranged the mussels on the half shell in a shallow baking dish, covered them with the stuffing and baked them in a 350 to 400 degree oven for about 20 minutes.

Note: You can do quahogs the same way. Great!

Moules Glacees

Simplicity is definitely not the keynote for Moules Glacées. There are several steps in preparing them, but your patience in following the proper procedure will result in a memorable entree.

First make the sauce:

THICK CREAM SAUCE

¼ cup butter	1 cup light cream
¼ cup flour	½ teaspoon salt
	½ teaspoon pepper

Melt butter and stir in flour until smooth. Gradually add cream and stir constantly until mixture boils and thickens. Cook about 5 minutes longer, stirring occasionally. Add salt and pepper.

Makes 1 cup sauce

Now back to the mussels. You will need, besides the cup of thick cream sauce:

4 pounds mussels, scrubbed	2 cups light cream
4 shallots, chopped	2 tablespoons butter
Salt and pepper	6 tablespoons whipped cream
2 cups dry white wine	

Place the well-scrubbed mussels in a saucepan with the shallots, salt and pepper, and wine. Cook, covered, for 10 minutes, or until the shells open. Remove the mussels from the wine mixture.

Take off the upper shell of each mussel and arrange the bottom shells containing the mussels in a single layer on a heatproof dish.

Cook the wine mixture over a low heat for 20 minutes more. Blend in the cream and the cream sauce you have made. Add the butter, a little at a time, stirring constantly. Boil for 4 or 5 minutes.

Remove this from the heat and add whipped cream. Pour this sauce mixture over the mussels. Broil about 8 inches from the heat for 2 or 3 minutes, or until the mussels are well browned.

Makes 4 servings

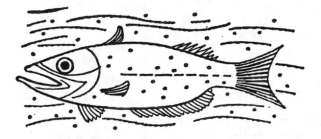

Of all of the fish in the sea off the coast
Most all of them cheerfully boast
That their flavor and savor
Find preference and favor
With host after host after host.

IV

THE ALMOST COMPLEAT ANGLERY: THE GULF OF MAINE FISH

" I love any discourse of fish and fishing . . . "
— The Compleat Angler, Isaak Walton

There really is no such word as anglery—at least I couldn't find it in any dictionary I have. But it suits my purpose admirably and can't be misunderstood: it's where the fish are, zillions of them. There are smelts and swordfish, mackerel and tuna, herring and haddock, flounders and pollock, cod, stripers, hake, ocean perch, alewives—you name them and the odds are they're somewhere around in the Gulf of Maine. There are no pompano or red snapper, mighty few blues, and the shad that once came up our rivers are long gone. However, there's enough variety to satisfy the most enthusiastic fish eaters and enough recipes extant to keep them eating a different fish dish twice a day for half a normal lifetime!

As with other seafoods, the Maine ways of cooking fish are basically simple. Naturally some seasoning is necessary, and an occasional onion helps, but freshly caught fish, cleaned and cooked within a few short hours, needs no outside support for its native goodness; its own flavor and substance are gratifying enough.

The nice thing about fish recipes is that practically every kind of fish, fresh, salt, or smoked, can be used in any of them. Fry them, boil them, bake them, broil them; cover them with sauces: they are the most accommodating and satisfying of comestibles. Good for you, too.

43

Cook fish short is the rule. Overcooking fish is worse than overbroiling a steak: the fish is not worth eating.

These few recipes and methods are honest guides to the full enjoyment of fish. Most of them are easy to put together and cook; all of them are sometime products of Maine kitchens.

The Maine Fish Chowder

Fish chowder, like clam chowder, should be carefully concocted and definitely not thickened with anything. The ingredients and the procedure are the same and the end result as flavorful and hearty. Either cod or haddock may be used, fillets or the whole fish. I think the whole fish gives the chowder a more sea-going taste.

Either way you do it, this is what you will need for 4 to 6 servings:

¼ pound salt pork, diced	1 teaspoon salt
3 onions, sliced fine	¼ teaspoon pepper
4 cups diced raw potatoes	1 quart rich milk
3 pounds fresh fish with bones	1 tablespoon butter
or 2½ pounds of fillets	

Making it with fillets is easier. After trying out the salt pork until it is crisp and brown, add onions, and sauté slowly. Put in water and potatoes and cook for 10 minutes, then add the fish (cut into good-sized pieces) and cook until it is tender. Add the seasonings, milk, and butter, and bring just to the boiling point.

Using a whole fish involves simmering it separately first with a bit of salt. (This is to keep the fish from breaking up.) When the fish is cooked, remove the bones and keep it in as large chunks as possible. Strain the fish stock. Now put the fish and the fish stock into the pot with the onions and potatoes, add the seasonings, milk, and butter, and bring just to the boiling point.

Makes 4-6 servings

Or Use Smoked Fish

I tried this variation one day and found it very interesting. Just use smoked cod or smoked haddock and prepare the chowder in the same manner as for the chowder with fillets.

Cod's Head Chowder

A concoction of the Coffin family, cod's head chowder begins with salt pork. Fry it in the kettle until it's dark brown, then throw in onions and fry them brown. Douse in some water and bring it to a boil. Sliced or diced potatoes are next. When they're boiling, in go very fresh young cod, heads and all, with only the eyes extracted. When the fish begins to flake apart, put the kettle on the back of the stove and add scalded milk—as much as you think is right. Pour it slowly and keep stirring. It needs 20 minutes for the flavor to develop. Then toss in common crackers and salt and pepper to taste.

If you could wait two days to eat it, so much the better!

Fried Fish

Probably more fish is fried in Maine than cooked in any other way. And there isn't a fish caught here that isn't skillet material.

Fry small fish whole, leaving on the heads and tails. Cut large fish fillets into fair-sized strips. They can be fried plain or dipped into an egg and milk mixture, then rolled in salted flour, corn meal, or fine cracker crumbs.

Put them into a hot skillet in about 1/8 inch of melted salt pork fat. Brown on one side, turn and brown the other, allowing 8 to 12 minutes total cooking time. (It will depend on the thickness.)

One of my favorite breakfasts is a mess of slivered baby pollock or herring fried in corn meal. (Slivers are solid strips of flesh cut off each side of the fish.)

Sadie Nason's Baked Haddock

Our friend Sadie can turn her hand to most anything: sewing, painting, paper hanging, rug braiding, Christmas wreath making. And she makes about the finest pies I've ever eaten. But that is only one small item in her culinary closet. Here's another, simple but downright good.

Chop an onion fine and spread out on the bottom of a flat, buttered baking dish. Lay fillets of haddock on top. Season. Bake for 20 or 25 minutes.

I'm sure it's not exclusive with Sadie, but that doesn't make any difference. And, by the way, cod or flounder do just as well.

Scrambled Fish

Try this for breakfast sometime, using salt or fresh fish. (Freshen the salt fish, or use cooked fresh fish.)

Put a couple of tablespoons of butter in a good-sized skillet, add 1 cup shredded fish, and when it begins to brown pour in a cup of milk. Cook for a few minutes, then add 3 well-beaten eggs. Season and stir until it is done like scrambled eggs.

Serves 4

Fish Balls or Cakes

It depends on how you want to fry them as to whether they are balls or cakes. The ingredients are the same.

1 cup cooked fish	1 tablespoon melted butter
1½ cups mashed potatoes	Pepper and salt to taste
1 egg, beaten	½ teaspoon onion juice
Fine bread crumbs	

Use any cooked, flaked fish you happen to have around the house—or cook some. Mix the first six ingredients together and form into balls or cakes. Then roll them in finely sifted dry bread crumbs. Sauté them if you've made flat cakes. Deep-fry them if they are balls. Either way they eat well, with or without a sauce.

(Ketchup's good.) And you won't be cheating if you use the modern, dehydrated mashed potatoes. They make it easier.

Makes 3-4 servings

Maine Boiled Fish Dinner

There are two schools: the salt-fish advocates and the fresh-fish supporters. I take neither side. One or the other, it's a sound, robust meal.

These are the usual ingredients in addition to the fish, but there is no reason why you can't use other—or more—vegetables: carrots, for instance, or turnips.

6 onions	¼ pound diced salt pork
6 potatoes	1½ cups hot white sauce
12 small beets	2 hard-cooked eggs, diced

For salt fish, use a 1½ or 2-pound salt cod. Cut the fish into serving portions. Freshen for 2 or 3 hours in cold water. Drain, cover with fresh water and bring to a boil. Drain. Meanwhile, the vegetables should have been cooking separately. Now fry the salt pork until brown. Arrange the fish on a hot platter and cover with a white sauce to which the diced, hard-cooked eggs have been added, and garnish with the crisp salt pork. Arrange the vegetables around the edges. It looks nice that way.

With fresh fish, wrap a 3-pound cod in cheesecloth or greased cooking parchment. Fill a deep saucepan 2/3 full of water and add ½ teaspoon of salt and 1 tablespoon of vinegar for each quart of water, to keep the fish firm. Put the fish in, making sure it's completely covered, and bring the water to a boil. Skim and reduce heat, letting it simmer, covered, until tender. Then serve with vegetables and sauce, as above.

Will serve 6

Groundfish, Maine Style

You have a lot of leeway in the kind of fish you use for this.

1½ cups cooked, flaked fish: haddock, finnan haddie, cod, smoked cod, halibut	Sprinkling of celery salt Salt to taste
2 hard-cooked eggs, separated	Salt pork fat and diced pork scraps
¼ teaspoon paprika	2 cups cooked rice

Combine the fish, chopped egg whites, and seasonings, and heat in the melted salt pork fat with the scraps, tossing often to prevent burning. Pile the hot cooked rice on a platter, toss the hot fish over the rice and garnish with diced egg yolks and parsley.

Serves 4 to 6

Easy Skillet Fish Dish

A meal in itself and one with a lot of oomph. I found it in a cookbook called "Maine-ly Recipes" put out by the P. T. A. of Harpswell, of which, if you don't know, Orr's Island is a part.

Flounder fillets are particularly good in this dish, but you can use cod or haddock as well.

¾ cup uncooked rice	Salt to taste
1 cup chopped celery	2½ teaspoons pepper
3 carrots, sliced	1½ cups water
½ cup chopped onion	Fish fillets
1 #303 can of tomatoes	Paprika
2 tablespoons butter	

In a 10-inch skillet place the rice, celery, carrots, onion, tomatoes, and butter. Stir in the salt, pepper, and water. Bring to a boil, cover and cook over low heat for 14 minutes, stirring once. Uncover and lay fillets over the mixture and sprinkle them with paprika. Cover and leave over low heat for 15 minutes, or until fish is done and the moisture absorbed.

This should serve 3 or 4

Fish Pudding

A casserole dish that glorifies creamed fish.

Gently boil a 5- or 6-pound haddock. Carefully remove all bones and shred the fish quite fine.

Stir ½ cup of flour smooth in 1 cup of cold milk, and set aside.

Let 1 pint of milk, ¼ onion, diced, and some minced parsley come to a boil over low heat; then slowly stir in the flour-milk mixture. Cook and stir until the sauce thickens. Slightly beat the yolks of 2 eggs and add. Season with ½ teaspoon of white pepper, add ¼ cup of butter, and salt well.

Butter a casserole and put in first a layer of sauce, then one of fish, and so on, finishing with a layer of sauce. Sprinkle cracker crumbs and a light grating of cheese on top. Bake for 30 minutes in a moderate oven (350 degrees).

Makes 6-8 servings

Finnan Haddie or Smoked Cod

The two fish are interchangeable here. I suppose, to make the cod lose some of his inferiority complex, we ought to call him finnan coddie. At any rate, the following verse seems appropriate.

THE HADDOCK THINKS HE'S BETTER THAN THE COD°

The haddock is often quite snooty
To the cod in the depths of the sea.
It's not that he thinks he's a beauty:
It's what he calls his destiny.

It began off of Scotland, oh long years ago,
When they caught him and brought him ashore,
They washed and they cleaned him above and below
And smoked him then smoked him some more.

In the land where golf started somewhere on a dune
And there came into being the caddie,
Smoked haddock became widely known very soon
And they gave it the name finnan haddie.

So the haddock feels he's a superior fish,
Though the cod takes of this a dim view.
For smoked cod, when it's cooked, is as tasty a dish:
Finnan could be his given name too.

Thus the codfish's nose is a bit out of joint,
While the haddock looks right down his snout.
There's no way that I know of to show them the point:
They're equals. Let them argue it out.

Regardless of how the fish feel, either smoked cod or finnan haddie will do nicely as follows:

My favorite is baked in milk and served with the same white sauce used in the Fish Pudding given on page 49. Just put the fish in a baking dish with milk to barely cover, and a sprinkling of salt. Ten or 15 minutes in a 300 degree oven does it. Make plenty of the sauce.

Broiled Finnan Haddie

Broiled finnan haddie or smoked cod is good, too. Cover the fish with hot water and let it stand 10 minutes. Drain it and place on a greased broiler rack. Spread with butter, sprinkle lightly with pepper, and cook under preheated broiler in moderate heat until brown, turning once. Serve with melted butter.

* From a series of verses, "Fish Have Their Problems Too," by the author.

Mackerel

If you have never had a tinker mackerel, you have missed a real treat. Tinkers are the babies, weighing from half a pound to a pound each. My love for them goes back to the days when Will Merriman set his nets in Ash Cove and appeared at our door before breakfast with all we could eat at two for a nickel. There has never been a brook trout or any other fish to beat it! And this is not a long-time memory speaking: it's as recent as this very day.

Cooking them is easy. Fry them in salt pork fat or butter, with or without flour, corn meal or crumbs. Bake them in milk. Or dot them with butter and broil them. (I prefer them split down the back.) They want no sauce. Eat them as they come out of the pan or off the rack and revel in their tender goodness.

They are great broiled over charcoal. For this you need one of those racks you use for cooking hamburgers. Grease it well and lock them in tight. Dot with butter and let the charcoal embers do the rest.

Larger mackerel are good too. Stuff and bake them as pollock (which recipe follows), or broil them. Fillet them and cut up the fillets and fry them. Keep it simple: that's how they taste best.

Then There Are Horse Mackerel Steaks

Tuna, tunny, or horse mackerel, it's all the same. You may recall that the Bailey Island Tuna Tournament, held every summer, is a big event, attracting crowds of sports fishermen from all over the country. Because tunas have migratory habits you don't always have them handy. In fact, they were scarce around here for a number of years but have now returned in large numbers and large sizes. And both the local harpooners and the sports-loving rod and reelers are mighty happy.

A 500-pound tuna fish is a profitable day's work for a professional fisherman. Almost daily during the summer season, one or more are hoisted onto Merrill's Wharf, weighed, and prepared for market.

Just about everyone on the islands fries tuna fish as he would a steak. Phil Johnson, storekeeper and fire chief on Bailey Island, uses a piece of salt pork in the skillet to "grease it up." "Don't cook it too long," he says, "when the color changes, it's done." Some parboil it first, to get rid of the oily taste.

The meat is rich and full of flavor and welcomed here as a very special meal.

Baked Stuffed Pollock

Pollock, like cod and haddock, are plentiful in our waters, and they come in all sizes: small, medium, and large. Ideally, you catch one yourself somewhere this side of Halfway Rock Light, clean it on your way back, and have it in the oven as fast as you can. It should weigh about 4 pounds and can be filled with a well-mixed stuffing made of

1½ cups bread crumbs	1 teaspoon poultry seasoning
¼ teaspoon salt	2 tablespoons melted fat
½ cup milk	

Or, if you have another favorite stuffing, use that.

Wipe the fish dry inside and out. Rub the inside well with salt. Stuff the fish and sew the edges together or lace them with string and toothpicks. Place it in a greased baking dish that can be used for serving at the table. Slash through the skin in several places—it helps to reduce shrinkage—and fasten on strips of salt pork 1½ inches apart. Pour 1 cup of rich milk over it. Bake 1 hour in a slow to moderate oven, basting occasionally with the milk in the pan. When done, pour off the milk into a saucepan and add enough more to make 1½ cups. Blend and cook 3 tablespoons of flour with the milk for a creamy gravy to serve over potatoes or other vegetables.

Serves 4-6

The Sole of Maine: Flounder

Hand-lining for flounder at full tide over the sand bar off Bar Island was one chore I welcomed as a boy. There were only six feet of water and you could watch the little fellows hook themselves and be pulled up.

Fried, sautéed, baked, or broiled whole, flounder is, in my opinion, just about as fine as tinker mackerel or trout. The meat is firm and nicely textured, white and toothsome. Filleted, they can be fancied up a bit, if you want, and made into exceptional dishes. Here's one my wife serves frequently and with unfailing success:

2 pounds flounder fillets	¼ cup dry white wine
2 tablespoons butter	1 tablespoon minced parsley
1 medium onion, chopped	1 tablespoon flour
1 clove garlic, minced	¼ teaspoon oregano
1 #2 can tomatoes	1 tablespoon heavy cream

(Actually there is a dish very similar to this in one of the local Maine cookbooks. The only difference is the wine. So leave it out if you must be a complete Maine conformist. I refuse to.)

Cut the fillets into serving pieces. Melt 1 tablespoon of the butter in a skillet, add the onion and garlic. Place the fillets on top and cover with the tomatoes, wine, and parsley. Let the liquid come to a boil, then cover the pan, lower the heat, and simmer for 10 to 15 minutes.

Remove fish to hot platter and keep it hot.

Cream the remaining tablespoon of butter with 1 tablespoon of flour and add to the sauce. Put in oregano and cook, stirring, for 5 minutes. Blend in heavy cream.

Pour sauce over fish and serve at once. The compliments will ensue immediately.

Makes 4-6 servings

Mother Coffin's Baked Fall Smelts

This is the way her son, Robert, wrote it:

The fulling and rounding time of the year is the only proper time to have your smelts right and to bring out their toothsomeness in cooking. The Fall is the right season. My mother's dish I am going to give you is tied in with the season when maple trees become bonfires, the frost flower stars the earth just ahead of the flowers of the frost itself, and the bays are covered with red-and-gold carpets of leaves that have fallen in all their glory into the tide. My mother was like that. She always tied herself into the seasons. She knew where she was every minute of the time. She knew her way about the seasons. Fall meant smelts. That was that. It was the law.

Mother Coffin baked the smelts whole—head, tail, and innards. First she took a chunk of salt pork and ran it all over a hot baking pan. Each smelt was slightly dusted with flour and placed side by side, nose to nose, and tail to tail—as many tiers as there were smelts. Then she cut a slab of salt pork into slender ribbons and laced it back and forth across the top at right angles to the fish. Then into the hot oven on an upper shelf they went for a good half hour. They are done, as Coffin put it, " when they look like a slab of medium mahogany."

Take them out with a spudger (perforated spatula) and eat them entire. You'll understand quickly why they're labeled " Baked Ambrosia."

While there's no doubt they are best in the fall, there's no reason I know of why they can't be enjoyed almost as much at other times of the year. I testify that they can!

Old-Time Pickled Herring

Three days ago, Sadie Nason came down to the house with a couple of dozen just-caught herring, and I pickled them forthwith. Before lunch today I opened a jar and tried them. Trudy had taken sort of a dim view of the project, but one taste convinced her, and between us, the contents of the jar disappeared. While the herring are running I'm going to make up a couple of jugs and put them down in the coolest part of the cellar for safekeeping. Then next New Year's Day I'll have my own herring to observe an old custom with.

Either fresh or salt herring can be used. The latter must be put into a flat glass or pottery dish with a quart of water, covered, and kept in a cool place for 12 hours, then drained and rinsed.

To prepare, loosen the back bone with ribs attached at the head end and pull them out intact. (The heads and tails have already been removed.) Cut away the thin flesh along the belly, and discard. Then cut the trimmed fish into inch wide, crosswise pieces. Arrange fish and ¼ inch onion slices in alternate layers in a jar, with a smattering of pickling spices each time. When the jar is full, combine ¼ cup of sugar, ¾ cup of cider vinegar, and 3 tablespoons water and pour in. Press onion and fish down so they're fully covered, seal, and store in a cool place for 2 or 3 days. Then they'll be ready for you.

There's no question that Maine fish are gastronomic aristocrats whose flavor and firm tenderness are worth a special trip Down East. As a realist, I know this is not always possible, but there's nothing to prevent your treating fish from other waters with the same understanding that we give them here. They'll be worthy table fare. So go to it with the altruistic blessings of this noble state.

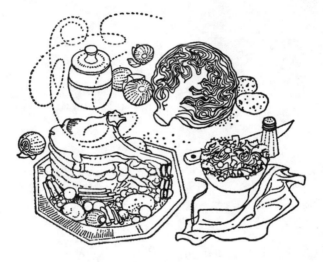

When it comes to meat and potatoes and such
Down in Maine they are treated with much
    Love and respect
    And thus always reflect
A robustious, gastronomical touch.

V

MEAT AND POTATOES, POULTRY AND SUCH

Hard roads, automobiles, and supermarkets have changed the face of Maine as they have all other sections of the country. Life has opened up considerably, but like the weather, the basic nature and way of living remain the same. A wide variety of foods is available today, and in most homes gas and electric stoves have replaced wood and coal stoves. Yet the ways of preparing and cooking food have changed little. It's just easier to do it.

As has been said, recipes are only suggestions. Cooking is an art, not a science, and it only comes alive in the doing and living with it, not by reading about it. The following dishes can thus become, in your kitchen, as worthwhile in substance and flavor as they have always been in Down East kitchens. For here are the experience and the living with and the ingredients.

Salt Pork

The backbone of Maine cookery is salt pork; it is used in more ways than you can count. It is the basic frying fat. Pork scraps add character to all sorts of dishes. And boiled with greens and potatoes, not to mention its importance in the bean pot, it does wonderful things to bring out the flavors of its companions. Without salt pork Maine cooking might well fall on its face!

Certainly Maine meat, vegetable, and poultry cooking is not limited to the few recipes detailed here. These are, however, good examples of the sound, unadorned methods that go into the preparation of Maine dishes. Neither perfuming the rose nor gilding the lily are Down East ways.

59

Salt Pork Gravy

If you have never had potatoes, mashed or baked, smothered with salt pork gravy, you have something really special to look forward to. In Maine it's as much a staple as the potato itself and, I am sure, one of the reasons people smile most of the time. (It's good on some vegetables, too.)

¾ pound salt pork	3 cups milk
	4 tablespoons flour

Dice the salt pork and fry it until it is brown and crisp. Remove the scraps and drain off all but ¼ cup of the fat. Add the flour and blend until smooth. Pour in the milk gradually, stirring constantly, until it boils and thickens. Simmer 5 minutes more, stirring occasionally. When it's ready, put back the pork scraps and pour into a gravy boat or bowl. Then watch the faces around the table. You'll have your reward right then and there.

Serves 5

Haskell Island Corn Chowder

One of the most beautiful islands in Casco Bay was formerly the summer home of my friends, Mal and Helen Jones. And this is her " rule," a chowder as beautiful as the island where it was served by the gallon when Maine corn came in. While there's no doubt it is best with fresh corn, it can be made with canned. As Helen says:

Try out some tiny cubes of salt pork and put aside. Pour off most of the fat and sauté a large chopped onion in it. Add one can of cream-style corn and stir, then add milk and evaporated milk (half and half) to right consistency. Must not be too thin. I am apt to put in more evaporated milk than regular milk, for it makes it richer. Serve with the pork scraps in it.

My advice is, don't stint on the pork scraps! Put in plenty.

Serves 4

Grandma Willan's Boiled Dinner

The food that came out of my grandmother's kitchen was monumental. Her Saturday production alone was enough to stock a small bakery and feed a squad of hungry Boy Scouts. She cooked as she lived, simply, wholesomely, and economically. While everything she turned out was great, I think of her boiled dinner as her finest achievement.

It was an unhurried, orderly procedure. The corned beef had to cook so long—usually something over 3 hours. She started it in cold water to which she added a few peppercorns.

Next she cut a head of cabbage into wedges and put it on the stove to simmer with a 2-pound chunk of salt pork which she scored with a knife. She cooked it for about two hours.

Meanwhile, she prepared the vegetables, peeling them all and quartering all but the onions, which were left whole:

3 parsnips	8 small onions
3 turnips	6 potatoes
6 large carrots	

When the corned beef was done she removed it from the pot and put in the parsnips, turnips, carrots, and onions. These simmered in the stock for 30 minutes, then the peeled and quartered potatoes were added, and the simmering continued for another 15 minutes. Finally she reheated the beef with the vegetables.

The hot corned beef and salt pork finally met on a platter and were surrounded with the vegetables, and the dinner was ready.

Today there are many short cuts in cooking meat and vegetables: in pressure cookers, for instance. By all that's holy don't do it with this. There is no short cut to the results my grandmother got: you can't improve on perfection, so don't try to.

Makes 6-8 servings

The Pork Boiled Dinner

Actually I think this was the original Maine boiled dinner. It stands to reason it was, for practically everybody years ago raised a hog or two. It was the only meat always on hand (except for chickens).

The procedure is the same as my grandmother's. The cut of pork can be most anything: the end of the loin, knuckles, ends, chops, hocks, jowl butts. Boil it until it's done and serve it as above.

Either way, a boiled dinner in Maine is eating of the finest kind: a substantial meal for substantial people.

Captain Will Sylvester's Pork Stew

A pot of pork stew on the back of the Sylvester stove was pretty much a fixture in the house. Bill Jr. told me that as a boy together with his brothers and sister, when they'd come in out of the cold they'd dip into it and eat their fill. That's what it was there for: to be eaten when they were hungry—morning, noon, afternoon, or night.

Its simplicity didn't lessen its solid goodness. Captain Will used any lean pork, boiling it in a big iron pot until it was almost done. Then he added quartered potatoes and whole onions and let it simmer until they were cooked. The longer it sat on the back of the stove, the better it was. But Bill assured me it didn't sit there very long. It seemed to him that his father had to replace it at least every other day. Could be—it's that good!

Pork Chop Casserole

Featured some years ago by Eddy the Eater in the "American Magazine," together with other Maine recipes, it was one of Mildred Powers's recipes.

6 pork chops (center cut or
    pork steak)
2 medium-size onions, sliced
6 medium-size potatoes, sliced

2 tablespoons flour
2 teaspoons poultry seasoning
Salt and pepper to taste

The casserole and the casserole lid (this is important) must be thoroughly greased with butter. Place three of the pork chops in the bottom and sprinkle them with salt and pepper and 1 teaspoon of the poultry seasoning. Place a layer of sliced onions, then a layer of potatoes on the chops and over these sift one tablespoon of the flour and a sprinkle of salt and pepper. Repeat the layers and seasonings, ending with a layer of potatoes on top. Fill the casserole to the top layer of potatoes with cold water.

Make a sauce as follows:

6 soda crackers
½ cup boiling water
2 tablespoons butter

1 teaspoon chopped onion
½ teaspoon poultry seasoning
Salt to taste

Crumble the crackers and soak the crumbs in the boiling water. Stir in the butter while the mixture is warm. Add the remaining ingredients and mix thoroughly. Spread this on top of the potatoes in the casserole, cover the casserole with the heavily greased lid, and bake 2¼ hours at 350 degrees, removing the lid for the last 30 minutes.

Serves 6

Mr. Bean's Bean Soup (Camp Style)

L. L. Bean of Freeport (see chapter on deer meat and other game) gave me several recipes that he has used in camp for years. They're every bit as good made at home, and easier to produce.

For his bean soup, soak one cup of beans overnight. Drain, and add 2 cups of fresh water. Pare and dice 2 medium-size potatoes and 1 medium-size onion, and add to the pot. Chop fine ¼ pound of salt pork and fry until brown, then add to the pot.

Salt and pepper lightly. Place the pot on stove and boil for 1 hour. Simple and hearty.

Serves 4

Mr. Bean's Pea Soup

Place 1 cup of split peas and a ham bone in a kettle and cover with water. Let simmer until peas and meat are well done, this requiring about 3 hours. Remove the bone and strain the peas. Remove bits of meat from the bone and add to the soup. Thin with milk if too thick.

This is enough for four people, one generous serving each.

And Mr. Bean's Camp Potatoes

¼ pound salt pork	8 medium-size potatoes
4 medium-size onions	

Fry the salt pork in a frying pan until crisp. Remove the pork. Dice the onions and fry until soft. Dice the potatoes, add them to the onions, and cook in covered pan until done. Remove the cover and brown. Add the cooked salt pork after chopping it very fine. Do not stir. Turn when brown on the bottom. Salt and pepper to taste.

Says Mr. Bean: "Quantity enough for one meal for four hungry campers."

Spiced Pot Roast

Marion Harris, several of whose recipes are Maine classics, found this in a very old local cookbook and has served it many a time. She claims it has done as much as anything else to build her reputation as a first-rate cook.

4 pounds beef	½ teaspoon salt
½ cup flour	½ teaspoon pepper
5 whole cloves	½ cup water
2 bay leaves	½ cup vinegar
2 large onions	3 large potatoes

Rub meat with flour and brown on all sides. Stick the cloves into the meat, throw in the bay leaves, slice the onions in over the meat. Add the salt and pepper, water and vinegar, and simmer for 3 hours. When meat is nearly done, slice the potatoes and put them in the pot. Cook until done.

Serves 6-8

Lamb, Beef, or Veal Pie

For a left-over meat dish this is one of the best. Maybe it's the biscuits on top that do it.

Cut up the meat into reasonably sized pieces. For 1 to 2 cups meat, you need ½ cup cooked celery, ½ cup peas, a sliced onion, salt and pepper. Put all this into a casserole. Then make a white sauce with ½ cup of flour and 2 cups of milk. Pour over. Then put biscuits on top for the crust.

Make your biscuit dough out of 1½ cups of flour, 4 teaspoons of baking powder, 1 teaspoon of salt, 1 cup of milk, 1 cup of shortening. Mix and roll out medium-size biscuits. Bake in a 400 degree oven until biscuits are brown.

Serves 4

Brunswick (Maine) Beef Stew

A good beef stew is as typical of Maine as it is of anywhere else. There's nothing especially Down East about this one: it's much like every other good old-fashioned country beef stew. It has a considerable sturdiness about it that will take solid care of the hungriest man or boy you can find.

3 pounds cubed stew beef	1 tablespoon salt
2 tablespoons salt pork fat	Pepper
2 large onions, sliced	1 bay leaf
2 garlic cloves, minced	1 cup peas
1 cup chopped celery	12 carrots
¼ cup chopped parsley	12 small onions
2½ cups canned tomatoes	6 potatoes, quartered
1 teaspoon thyme	½ cup flour

If you haven't any salt pork to try out, use bacon fat or cooking oil. Brown the meat well, add the sliced onions, garlic, celery, parsley, tomatoes, thyme, salt, pepper, bay leaf, and 2½ cups water. Bring to a boil, reduce heat, cover, and simmer for 2 hours. Add remaining vegetables and simmer for 1 hour. Blend flour with ¾ cup of cold water and stir into stew. Simmer for five minutes.

6 very generous servings .

Steak in the Skillet

Broilers are comparatively modern parts of stoves and very handy too. But to this day most steaks in Maine are well salted and peppered, slapped into a piping hot, ungreased skillet, and done to a turn on top of the stove. Rare, medium or well done; rump, sirloin, porterhouse, or round; this is the way they're cooked. And I can tell you the meat is as juicy and flavorful as you'll ever want. Saves cleaning the broiler, too.

Paul Bunyan's Fire Box Steak

Ned Buxton, who among other things, worked one time in a Maine lumber camp, tells of cooking tremendous steaks in the fire box of a logging locomotive. Because Paul Bunyan was a Mainer and obviously had a tremendous appetite, these steaks were named for him.

The steak was placed on the coal shovel and held over the fiery coals until one side was seared. Then the trick was to pull it out and flip it over by tossing it in the air. There's no admitted record of any misses.

Of course, even if anyone wanted to do this there are few engines left that burn wood or coal. So this may be labeled a lost culinary art. It's just as well.

Chicken a la Chamberlain

The "Good Cooking" column in the Brunswick Record featured this turn-of-the-century recipe that was a favorite of General Joshua L. Chamberlain, the hero of Little Round Top at Gettysburg.

As the story goes, what with Harriet Beecher Stowe writing "Uncle Tom's Cabin" in Brunswick and General Chamberlain receiving General Lee's sword at Appomattox, the Civil War is said to have begun and ended in Brunswick.

The General, after the war, became President of Bowdoin College and Governor of the State. His home on Maine Street was an hospitable place and his dinners were famous.

He delighted in joking about the good and not-so-good cooks who made the dumplings that surrounded his stewed chicken. His chuckling remarks about the rocks or buckshot that must be in them prompted the household cook to try a new trick: placing lightly toasted shredded wheat biscuits, then a novelty, around the bird instead of dumplings. Mrs. Winfield Smith, who was once employed in the Chamberlain home, tells us the story and gives us the recipe:

Start with a lusty rooster or prime fat hen, over a year old, preferably a Plymouth Rock. Wash out the cleaned and dressed bird thoroughly. Put about 2 quarts of water in a kettle large enough to hold a 4-5 pound bird. Add 2 onions, whole, cut up celery, salt to taste. Simmer until done, but not too long, or the bird will fall to pieces. It should be kept whole, to be carved at the table according to etiquette. Place the bird on a large, deep platter and surround with toasted shredded wheat biscuits. Pour the slightly thickened gravy over the biscuits. Garnish with parsley or other greens.

No potatoes are served with this meal, but side dishes of well-buttered green and yellow vegetables, relishes, pickles, and cranberries complete the menu. . . . . . The recipe calls for your prettiest finger bowls and finest damask napkins. I recall the exquisite bowls of colored, gemlike clear glass that held the fragrant water. In those days, even the men, carefully watching the women, dipped the tips of their fingers in the water, removing them so fast you'd think the water was charged with electricity. What a glorious time that era was, and I am so glad I was part of it.

Dumplings the General Would Have Liked

The late Mrs. Annie Douglass of South Harpswell, also in the Brunswick Record, offered the cure for General Chamberlain's weighty dumplings. Here is her more than a century-old family recipe for dumplings that never fail:
When cooking beef, lamb, or chicken, remove 1 cup of the broth before adding potatoes or vegetables. Allow this to cool and add 2 slightly rounded teaspoons of baking powder, and stir in all the flour it will take. (The broth provides the shortening and salt needed.) Dip your spoon in the kettle so the dough will not stick to it. Then drop spoonfuls of dough into the boiling kettle. Cover tightly and cook 8 minutes. If covered tightly these never fail. How can you go wrong?

Makes about 12 dumplings

Father Coffin's Dumplings

"The dumplings were my father's," wrote Robert P. Tristram Coffin:
He invented them . . . Imagine, if you can, eating macaroni that had been carefully split lengthwise and then all the strips sewn together by a thread not there into one piece of toothsomeness four inches wide. Imagine how, by some miracle, all the taste there is in a young five pound chicken had been gathered into this exquisite velvet that

melted away on your tongue! Imagine all that if you want to, but it won't do you a bit of good. My father's dumplings are the peaks to which macaroni's suavity is but the merest foothill. Macaroni at its softest and most resilient is only a poor imitation of these seraph feathers of our family . . . .

My mother remembered that red letter day. She had a chicken cooking in the iron kettle on the back of the stove. . . . She was rolling out piecrust on her bread board . . . You know how raw piecrust is. It is alive and runs and curls away from the slash you give it with a silver knife. Well, my father was watching, and suddenly he had an idea . . . He caught up a rose leaf of live piecrust and held it in his palm . . . And before my mother could stop him, he threw the lively and crimping leaf of crust right into the pot with the chicken . . .

It sank . . . But then the miracle happened. The piecrust rose. The thin ribbon of flour came gently to the surface. It floated. And it was a transformed thing. It was smooth as a panel of velvet. It had expanded. It had exploded internally. And when my father took it on the iron cooking spoon and bit into it, he bit into the Promised Land. All the taste in that chicken had risen and concentrated in that smooth and suave piece of educated flour and salt and water.

My sire went back of the piecrust. He seized the flour sifter himself . . . and he went to it. Piecrust had too much shortening in it, of course. He wanted a purer and more perfect thing. He mixed his flour with cold water and just a touch of salt and just the smallest dab of butter in the world, to make the dough into a more malleable substance . . . Then he seized the knife, slashed it into cringing rectangles and threw them like crumpled rose petals into the chicken pot.

They all settled to the bottom of the pot and never came up. They stuck all together. My father's face fell. But he dipped out the unsightly lump and began all over. He had seen his error. He fed the next lot in one at a time, and he let each rose leaf rise to the surface before he put in the next one . . . So he had done it . . . So our family dumplings came into being.

Baked Chicken Legs

There's a modern touch to this one: aluminum foil. I like the simplicity and brevity of Arlene Lubee's recipe:

Dip chicken legs in canned milk, roll in seasoned cornflake crumbs, place on cookie sheet lined with aluminum wrap, thick side up. Bake in 350 to 400 degree oven until brown. No need of turning.

Try the same with pork chops.

Any questions?

Chicken Pot Pie

They make chicken pot pies in various ways here. Somehow this one appeals to me most. I hope you'll agree.

1 large chicken (cut in portions)	3 large onions
	Salt and pepper
4 or 5 large potatoes	Pie dough

Place a layer of chicken in the bottom of a large iron kettle and cover with thick slices of raw potato, then slices of onion, and add salt and pepper.

Roll pie dough out rather thick and cut in 2-inch squares and place on top of the onion. Continue layers until kettle is full, having the top layer pie dough. Add enough water to cover the contents halfway. Cover kettle tightly and cook over a low flame until chicken is tender.

You'll find a recipe for pie dough, if you need one, in the Bakery Department. Or use a ready-mix.

Serves 4-6

Maine Chicken Barbecue

Chicken barbecues, like lobster festivals and lobster bakes, are regular affairs in Maine. And, if you don't know it, Maine chickens rank with Maine lobsters in quality, flavor, and downright goodness. It's big business too: sixty-two million chickens are produced every year along with fifty-five million dozen eggs.

This past year a big public barbecue was held in Belfast City Park on July 13. Barbecued chickens were served continuously from 10:30 to 4:30, all cooked over charcoal, the cooking pits ranging from here to there!

You can easily have your own chicken barbecue as we do quite often. This is the authentic recipe:

Get 2½ pound Maine broiler-fryers and halve them, allowing a half chicken per serving. Baste them with the famous and simple Maine barbecue sauce: 1 cup cider vinegar, 1 cup water, ½ cup cooking oil, salt to taste. (This is enough sauce for two birds.)

When the charcoal has turned gray, place chicken, well brushed with sauce, on grill, skin side up. Turn every six to eight minutes, basting side that is up at each turning. Chicken is done when crispy brown and drumstick twists out of thigh joint readily.

Kenneth Roberts's Bean-Pot Beans

Actually these were his grandmother's beans and were done very much like my grandmother's. I guess all grandmothers of that era made unforgettable baked beans. Mr. Roberts's recipe appeared in his book "Trending into Maine" together with a number of others, two of which appear in later chapters in this book (see index). Mr. Roberts wrote:

Makes 6 to 8 servings. My grandmother's beans were prepared like this:

4 cups small white beans	½ cup molasses
1 pound piece of salt pork	1 tablespoon salt
1 large peeled onion	1 teaspoon pepper
1 heaping teaspoon dry mustard	

1. Four cupfuls of small white beans were picked over to eliminate the worm-holed specimens and the small stones that so mysteriously intrude among all beans, then covered with water and left to soak overnight.

2. Early the next morning, usually around five o'clock, they were put in a saucepan, covered with cold water and heated until a white scum appeared on the water. They were then taken off the stove, the water thrown away, and the bean-pot produced.

3. In the bottom of the bean-pot was placed a one pound piece of salt pork, slashed through the rind at half-inch intervals, together with a large peeled onion; then the beans were poured into the pot on top of the pork and onion. On the beans were put a heaping teaspoon of mustard, half a cup of molasses, and a teaspoon of pepper; the bean-pot was filled with boiling water, and the pot put in a slow oven.

4. At the end of two hours, a tablespoon of salt was dissolved in a cup of boiling water and added to the beans. Every hour or so thereafter the cover was removed, and enough boiling water poured in to replace that which had boiled away.

5. An hour before suppertime, the cover was taken off for good, the salt pork pulled to the top, and no more water added. Thus the pork, in the last hour, was crisped and browned, and the top layer of beans crusted and slightly scorched.

6. When the beans were served, the pork was saved

and the scorched beans skimmed off and thrown away. The two great tricks of bean-making seemed to be the frequent adding of water up to the final hour of baking, so that no part of the beans had an opportunity to become dry, and the removal of the cover during the last hour.

Serves 6-8

The Sweets and The Unsweets—Beans, That Is!

Robert P. Tristram Coffin had very definite ideas about baked beans. As he said:

Finally, the sweetening. Here the roads divide. For in New England there are two camps. Everybody is in one or the other. There are no neutrals. The Sweets and the Unsweets. They are bitterly opposed to each other. Blows may be exchanged. No quarter is given. Houses, even, are split in two on this crucial point. Ours was, on the farm. My mother had to bake two different pots of beans every Saturday of her life in the country. There was no compromise possible . . . The sweet and the unsweet pots had to be rotated.

If you want to spoil your beans, if you wish to undo all the natural goodness in the universe . . . pour in now one half cup of thick molasses, and ruin everything. Join the Sweets and be forever cursed to remain on the lower level of culture. But if, like me, you are one of the Unsweets and wise, put in one tablespoon only of molasses—or, better still, one heaping one of brown sugar. This will be enough to give the thinnest edge of an exquisite suggestion of sweetness which the beans need to be perfect . . .

A very positive man was Mr. Coffin. My grandmother and Kenneth Roberts's grandmother used a half cup of molasses. Such was the perfection of their beans that I would hesitate to deviate one grain of salt from their formula, much less almost half a cup

74 MEAT AND SUCH

of molasses. I guess I am condemned to the lower level of culture in Mr. Coffin's book. So be it! I'll still eat them sweet, and you can do what you please about it.

Green Pig—Dandelion Greens and Salt Pork

In the spring of the year the dandelions are all over the place, tender green shoots that are yours for the picking. Now dandelion greens may seem to you to be totally undesirable. But have a care, for you have missed one of the greatest eating experiences there is if you've never had them.

Let Robert Coffin tell you:

Dandelion greens put the green into the man . . . But you must not eat dandelions as a side dish or a salad . . . This little cousin of the sun is to be cooked. And he is to become the center of the meal . . . the whole works. He is to be cooked as he has been traditionally cooked in northern New England and the deep South for generations . . . The small green pasture octopuses, once you have sliced them out of the earth and washed them in many waters . . . are to be crowded into an ancient iron kettle, with a half pound of salt pig in their midst, scored so that it will cook clear through and send out its savor into the greens.

Dandelion greens are to be boiled right up and down for three or four hours. I know modern dietitians will blanch and hold to the table till their knuckles show white . . . Let all the vitamins and mineral salts go up in steam and out of the kettle . . . You are after bigger game. You are after vegetables. You are after life. Something that will stick to your ribs. You are after iron and soul.

The taste of infant dandelion sprouts with salt pork cooked into them, boiled till they are tender as butter and melt as fast, is a taste for the emperors of earth . . . It re-creates a man. A man eats five plates of it, with a dash of vinegar on each green mountain . . . And after he has his dandelions in him, the man runs out on the hills, kicks up all four heels, and beats the ten-year-old boys at baseball.

There you have it! I have only one further suggestion: do as most of the people do around here—throw a few Maine potatoes in the pot for the last half hour or so. Then you'll really have a complete meal. You'll want nothing else at that sitting.

Do It With Other Greens, Too

While dandelion greens, like a spring tonic, are only available for a brief spell, try the same way of cooking beet greens, spinach, turnip greens, swiss chard, green beans. It's the preferred way around here for all greens and many vegetables, and in this case preferred means the finest.

FIDDLEHEADS, MILKWEED, AND OTHER ROADSIDE GREENS

Edible weeds, in addition to the dandelion, abound in the fields and alongside roads in Maine. Of them all probably fiddleheads and milkweed are the most widely used.

Fiddleheads appear early in the spring in wet places in the state—tender, little rolls of fern that should be broken from the plant almost as soon as they appear, with an inch or two of stalk. Brown scales and woolly covering must be brushed out and removed, then the heads are washed and cooked in a small amount of lightly salted boiling water until just tender (12 to 20 minutes). Serve them with hot salt pork fat or butter. The quicker they are eaten the more delicate their flavor. They may also be served on toast like asparagus. Two of the fiddleheads, the Ostrich Fern and the Cinnamon Fern, have begun to appear in markets of larger cities. Perhaps you will find some in your market.

Milkweed is a delicious green with a taste that is a cross between dandelion greens and spinach. It is best in the spring when the plants are new and tender, but can be used throughout the season. Pick the tender tops of the plant, wash, drain, and boil as you would any other green.

Cow-slip or Marsh Marigold, Plantain, Purslane or "pusley," and Pigweed are other weed wonders that find favor hereabouts, cooked as above.

THE GREAT MAINE POTATO

A little over a hundred years ago, lumber was king in northern Maine. It was the ·axe that transformed great forests to great fields and the Yankee, the Britisher, and the fast-moving immigrant who came to Maine to farm, soon discovered the soil and climate were ideal for producing fine-tasting, fine-textured potatoes. Today Maine produces about one-seventh of the total U. S. production. Maine potatoes lead the country in yield per acre and are the largest selling white potato in America (Advt.).

Thus you can no more ignore the Maine potato than you can the Maine lobster. They are of a piece: high in quality, distinctive in flavor, both true culinary aristocrats.

A lot of people here grow their own, as my father did those many summers at Ash Cove. Digging them was fun. Of course, we would spike a few with the prongs of the clam rake but that didn't hurt them any.

They're a staple food, all right. Hardly a meal is served without them—boiled, baked, fried, mashed, in hash, smothered with salt pork gravy or clam muddle or, yes, with lobster glop. Potato soups, potato pancakes, potato candy (see page 118), potato doughnuts (see page 102)—ah, the Maine potato, what a versatile chunk of goodness it is!

For deer meat and ducks, rabbits and birds,
The hunter has only the kindest of words.
    There's no need to explain
    That the game down in Maine
Comes in coveys and bevies and herds.

VI

DEER MEAT, DUCKS, AND OTHER GAME

Many men have reached the status of living legends, their achievements and philosophies becoming integral parts of their times and thus lasting influences on future generations. Such is L. L. Bean of Freeport, Maine—hunter, fisherman, manufacturer, merchant, and philosopher.

He has not only hunted and fished throughout the entire State of Maine—the happiest of hunting grounds—but has traveled far and wide to test his knowledge, skill, and equipment in the field, the forest, and on inland and coastal waters. Out of his long experience came important inventions and improvements in methods and accoutrements, which he developed and offered to the nimrods and Izaak Waltons of the whole country. The L. L. Bean Catalog is not only nationally known and distributed: it is an American classic and a full repository of practical head-to-toe clothing for sportsmen and the most efficient camping, hunting, and fishing accessories. Any hunter coming to Maine knows the L. L. Bean store, open 24 hours a day, 365 days a year.

In planning and writing "What's Cooking Down in Maine," I sought out Mr. Bean and asked his permission to use some of his recipes that have appeared in his book "Hunting, Fishing and Camping." Several appear in other chapters of this book. His game recipes are on following pages under appropriate headings.

VENISON OR MAINE BEEF

Theodore Roosevelt, a pretty fine hunter himself, once said that Maine deer are the outstanding specimens of their kind in the world. Mainers take such observations as only fitting. They know

79

that Maine deer deserve the same high kudos as the Maine lobster: they're that special!

I do not understand how anyone can turn up his nose at venison. " It's strong. It's gamey. It's tough " go the comments. So are certain kinds of beef and lamb, but you can't blame the whole cattle population for it.

Properly aged, prepared, and cooked Maine deer is one of the most delicious of meats. Steaks, cutlets, chops, roasts, haunches: each cut has its virtues and each can become a memorable eating experience in the hands of an understanding cook.

Down here almost every household has venison in large or small supply, and it is cooked and eaten with as much relish today as when, years ago, other fresh meat being hard to come by, it was a mainstay in the winter diet.

Here are Mr. L. L. Bean's ways with venison.

Venison Steak

Mr. Bean prefers a steak about 1½ inches thick. Remove excess fat and wipe clean and dry. Have a very hot fire and when the frying pan is smoking hot, drop the steak into the pan and allow to sear quickly on one side. Then turn.

If you like steak medium or well done, reduce the heat of the fire and turn occasionally until at desired stage. If you prefer a rare steak, it will require 10 to 12 minutes; if medium, 15 to 20 minutes.

Serve on a hot platter. Spread the steak with butter and add salt and pepper to taste. (Cook chops the same way.)

Venison Cutlets

Cut small slices of meat from the loin about 1¼ inches thick. Sprinkle with salt and pepper and brush with melted butter. Roll in bread crumbs. Fry in butter.

Roast Leg of Venison

Cut leg and a piece of the loin, which will weigh about 5 or 6 pounds. Wipe dry with a damp cloth. Sprinkle lightly with salt and pepper and roll in flour. Attach several strips of salt pork. Put in roaster and bake three hours.

Leona Schumaker's Roast Venison

This is not a traditional Maine method for cooking venison, but it is a method I highly recommend. For want of a better description, it is similar to a sauerbraten and is a very noble way to treat Maine deer meat. Whenever Leona visits us and there is venison available she exercises her virtuosity with it: a fine art, I might add!

It involves marinating the roast for 8 hours, using these ingredients:

1 large onion, chopped	½ teaspoon each sweet herbs
2 tablespoons chopped	Salt and pepper
spring onions	4 whole cloves
2 large carrots, chopped	1 cup tarragon vinegar
5 tablespoons olive oil	1 cup dry red wine

Fry the vegetables in the oil, adding the seasonings. Then combine with the vinegar and the wine in a bowl or pan large enough to accommodate the roast. Put in the roast and let it marinate, basting every 2 hours.

When ready to cook, sear the meat for 15 minutes in a 450-degree oven, then reduce heat to 350 degrees and roast for 1½ hours, basting frequently. (Use up all the marinade and be sure to pour it over the meat when serving.)

Venison with Sour Cream

2 pounds venison	1 teaspoon salt
1 clove garlic	Pepper
¼ cup fat	1 bay leaf
1 cup diced celery	2 cups water
½ cup minced onion	4 tablespoons butter
1 cup diced carrots	4 tablespoons flour
	1 cup sour cream

Cut the venison in pieces. Add meat and garlic to the fat in a heavy skillet. Brown on all sides and put into baking dish. Place vegetables in remaining fat in skillet and cook for 2 minutes. Add salt, pepper, bay leaf, and water. Pour over the meat and bake in a slow oven until meat is tender.

Melt the butter in a frying pan and stir in the flour. Add enough liquid from the meat pot to make about ½ cup, and boil until thick. Put in sour cream and more salt, if necessary. Pour over meat and vegetables and serve.

Serves 4-6

Moose Steak

If you've never had moose meat and if, by some remote happenstance, some friend of yours brings one down from Canada (they're legal there, not in Maine) and gives you a steak, here's one way of cooking it. The recipe is from a recent Orr's Island cookbook.

½ cup finely chopped onion	1 cup chopped mushrooms
2 tablespoons butter	2 tablespoons flour
	½ cup sweet or sour cream

Fry the onions in butter until brown. (An iron skillet is best.) Sear the steak on both sides in the browned onions and butter. Cover and simmer for ½ hour. When almost tender add the mushrooms, stir the flour into the cream, and add to the meat. Cover and let simmer until done.

Actually, a deer meat steak would do just as well. Or for that matter a beefsteak.

DUCKS

Merrymeeting Bay, at the mouth of the Kennebec River, is one of the most famous duck-hunting regions in the entire East. There are also many other salt-water bays and inlets as well as inland lakes and streams where ducks are plentiful, and thousands of hunters seek them.

The popular ducks are the Black, Scaup, Goldeneye, Ringneck and some Mallards.

Cooking duck is not difficult if you follow some very simple rules.

Mr. Bean's Roast Duck

Clean and dress the duck. Steam about 1½ hours before roasting. Stuff with sliced onion or apple. Sprinkle with salt and pepper and cover the breasts with several slices of salt pork. Bake about 20 minutes in a very hot oven, basting every 4 or 5 minutes with the fat in the pan. Remove the stuffing before serving.

Buck Parsons's Roast Duck

When Buck attended pre-med school he learned something about using a scalpel. (He gave up the idea of becoming a doctor.) He is an accomplished duck hunter and here's how he dresses and cooks his ducks.

If he doesn't have his scalpel handy he uses a razor blade to de-feather and skin the ducks, all in one operation. Every trace of fat clinging to the carcass is removed and the skinned duck placed breast up in an uncovered roasting pan. He dredges it with flour and fastens strips of salt pork over the breasts, and salts and peppers it. The oven must be piping hot and the duck should roast anywhere from 20 to 40 minutes, with frequent basting. (It's how you like it, rare or well done, that determines the roasting time.) Prick the duck deeply with a sharp fork, and if blood does not follow the fork it's done.

The skinning removes all traces of a strong taste in the meat. If you want, stuff it with an onion or two, removing them when serving.

Roast Pheasant

The simplest method and in many ways the best, according to Mr. Bean: Dress and clean the pheasant. Tie several pieces of fat bacon or salt pork on the breast. Bake 30 to' 50 minutes, basting frequently with fat in the pan. Remove bacon or salt pork before serving.

Smothered Pheasant

From "Good Home Cooking" in the Brunswick Record, this is a hearty, rib-sticking dish.

Cut the pheasant into serving pieces and soak overnight in salt water. Wipe dry. Shake in a paper bag with flour, salt, pepper, and paprika. Heat 2 tablespoons of salt pork fat or cooking oil in the frying pan. Brown the pheasant pieces well on all sides. Add 1 cup of sweet or sour cream (or more, depending on the amount of pheasant you have). Cover. Simmer slowly for 3 hours, or until tender. Less time is required if pheasants are young and tender. When done, remove meat, thicken gravy, and pour over the meat in a serving dish.

Try this with Rock Cornish Game Hen.·It won't be necessary to soak these in salt water first.

Larded Grouse

On each bird lay thin slices of salt pork until the bird is completely covered. Wrap with string to keep the pork in place. Put in a roasting pan and pour enough water over birds for basting. Roast 20 to 25 minutes at 400 degrees. Remove the strips of pork, brush the birds with melted butter, and place in the oven again until they turn a rich brown.

Mr. Bean's Fried Grouse

Skin and dress the grouse. Remove the legs. Cut the breast in half lengthwise. Break down flat the piece containing the breastbone. If you're in camp, do it with a camp axe or the back of a hunting knife. At home a mallet or the flat of a cleaver will do. Wipe with a damp cloth. Fry in pork or bacon fat. Season with salt and pepper when served.

Rabbit Stew with Dumplings

It was done this way on the Coffin farm and was a regular table feature in the winter—the oftener the better, according to Robert P. T.

Cut a plump, cleaned rabbit into serving pieces. Put them in an iron kettle and boil hard for an hour. Then test the meat with a fork, and if it's tender, salt and pepper it, stir in a handful of flour for thickening, cut up a small onion, and then make the dumplings.

Take a pint of flour, sift it and put in 1 teaspoon cream of tartar, ½ teaspoon of saleratus, ½ teaspoon of salt and mix it with sweet milk to a consistency that can be handled without getting stuck to it. Roll it on a bread board and cut pieces about the size of a teaspoon, dropping them into the stew one at a time, giving each one room before you put in the next. When they've blossomed out and soaked up all the goodness in the pot you're ready to serve it up, big plates full of just about the finest stew you've ever tasted.

The muffins and cookies and blueberry pies,
The puddings and doughnuts and yeast breads that rise,
   And other home bakin'
   Including the cake, in
Maine ovens can really be praised to the skies.

VII

THE BAKERY AND DESSERT DEPARTMENT

That wonderful old New England institution—home baking—is still very much an institution in Maine households. Every week their ovens bring forth a prodigious quantity of breads, muffins, biscuits, cookies, cakes, and pies. I dare say there are more recipes—and good ones—for baked goods than for any other cooking in Maine. And for the most part, the ingredients and procedures of other years are followed today. Short cuts and prepared materials are not generally countenanced. Baking is done with the same loving care, know-how, and patience that was given to it by the grandmothers and mothers of most of the women here. And the same is true of the homemade puddings and other desserts—from Kenneth Roberts's chocolate custards to Harpswell upside-down pudding.

While the barrel of flour, put in for the winter, is not much in evidence today, plain, ordinary flour is, prepared mixtures notwithstanding. When you come right down to it, there's a lot more satisfaction in creativeness than in enlisting the more or less mechanical assistance of ready-to-use mixes.

To detail all of the products and their preparation would alone fill a good-sized cookbook. I think, however, that the samples that follow are more than enough to keep you going: a wide enough variety to keep your family bakery- and dessert-happy for a considerable time.

THE MAINE BLUEBERRY

Blueberries are the most versatile of berries and in Maine they are all over the place—sweet and juicy with a wild flavor no cul-

89

tivated berry can ever attain. A dish of them covered with thick cream is not only a happy breakfast starter but a much-to-be-desired dessert for other meals.

I can remember picking them in Clarendon Bibber's fields. Mother paid me a nickel a quart, and most summers we'd have all we wanted for pies and cakes and muffins as well as innumerable quarts, packed in glass jars and sent home to New Jersey for winter enjoyment. And just this past summer, I found them in plentiful supply on Johnson's Point, the half mile of land that stretches down the Sound from the Pearl House.

Of all the blueberry confections, the pie was—and still is— my favorite. A pie made of Maine blueberries, picked the same morning, is one of the noblest culinary creations there is. Don't just take my word for it. Try it yourself. As I said, the berries are plentiful and easy to pick. You can, of course, find frozen or canned berries in the markets. They're second-best but satisfying when you treat them properly as in these recipes.

Sadie Nason's Blueberry Pie

Sadie has a masterful way with pie fillings and crusts. As I mentioned earlier, her pies defy description and of them all, her blueberry pie is the best: an unforgettable eating experience as it comes out of the oven piping hot and juicy to be served in great big wedges.

First there's the pie crust—and this you can use with every kind of pie.

2 cups flour	1 cup shortening
½ teaspoon baking powder	½ teaspoon salt

Knead together the above ingredients. When well mixed stir in cold milk gradually, until the dough comes clean from the bowl. (No sticking.) Sadie says the milk is the secret ingredient that makes her crusts so short and so brown. Roll the pastry out and line the bottom of your pie tin.

Now for the filling: put on top of the bottom dough 1 quart of blueberries, 1 cup of sugar, the juice of ½ lemon, a sprinkling of cinnamon, and 1 tablespoon of butter (in 1 lump in the middle).

Dab milk all around the edge of the lower crust before putting on the top crust (slashed in the center to let the air out as the pie bakes). The milk on the edge seals the pie so the juices sta/ in. Press all around the edge with a fork. Spread the crust with shortening and then milk. This, as Sadie says, makes it nice and brown.

And there you have it—just about the finest blueberry pie in the State of Maine and that could mean the world! Any challengers?

Makes 4–6 servings

Another Kind of Blueberry Pie

Like a pumpkin pie, this blueberry pie does nicely without a top crust but with a topping of ice cream or whipped cream. The recipe came from Helen Jones, my Haskell Island friend, and deserves high commendation. (Incidentally Haskell Island is loaded with blueberry bushes.)

1 9-inch pastry shell	2 tablespoons flour or
1 quart blueberries	1 tablespoon cornstarch
1 cup sugar	¼ teaspoon salt
¾ cup water	¼ cup of water

Dash of lemon juice, if desired

Bake a 9-inch pastry shell. Take out 3 cups of blueberries and put them aside. To the remaining berries add 1 cup of sugar and ¾ cup of water and cook until soft. Make a paste of the flour or cornstarch, salt, and cold water, and stir into the berries. Cook slowly until thickened. (Helen adds a bit of lemon juice at this point.) Add the hot mixture to the uncooked berries, cool a little, and pour into the pastry shell. Chill for 3 hours. Serve with ice cream or whipped cream topping.

Makes 6 servings

Margaret Chase Smith's Blueberry Cake

Senator Smith could serve this to the Democratic side of the Senate and accomplish in a trice what Dale Carnegie's book imparts: the winning of friends and influencing of people— though I'm sure she doesn't really need the help.

½ cup shortening	4 teaspoons baking powder
1 cup sugar	½ teaspoon salt
2 eggs	1 teaspoon nutmeg
2 cups sifted flour	1 cup milk
2 cups blueberries	

Cream the shortening, add the sugar, and beat until creamy. Add the eggs and beat until light and foamy. Mix together and sift the flour, baking powder, salt, and nutmeg, and add alternately to the creamed mixture with the milk. Fold in the blueberries. Bake in two well-greased 9- or 10-inch layer cake tins in a moderately hot oven, 375 degrees, for 25 to 30 minutes. Remove from the oven and allow to cool for 10 minutes in the tins. Then turn onto cake rack. When cool, put the layers together with frosting.

Blueberry Muffins

Perennial favorites here, they are as eagerly devoured at dinner as at breakfast.

2 cups sifted flour	1 egg, beaten
3 teaspoons baking powder	¾ cup milk
1/3 cup sugar	¼ cup shortening, melted
¾ teaspoon salt	1 cup blueberries

Mix and sift the dry ingredients. Mix together the egg, milk, and melted shortening, and add. Stir only enough to mix, then add the blueberries. Fill greased muffin tins or greased gem pans two-thirds full. Bake at 425 degrees for 20 to 25 minutes.

1-2 dozen muffins

Blueberry Cobbler

Ruth Doughty of Orr's Island offers this interesting dessert. The dough and the berries change places in the oven. Don't peek. It might not happen if you do.
Make a dough of these ingredients:

Walnut size piece of butter	2 teaspoons baking powder
1 cup flour	½ cup sugar
½ cup milk	½ teaspoon salt

Mix well and spread over bottom of a well-buttered baking dish. Then turn over on the dough: first, 2 cups of blueberries; second, a cup of sugar, and last, 1 cup of boiling water. Bake in a moderate oven 35 to 45 minutes. When it's done, the dough will be on top and the sauce underneath.

Lill's Blueberry Gingerbread

A pamphlet from the Maine Department of Agriculture features this recipe, which was known in Lill's family for more than fifty years as Delicious Gingerbread. It is!

½ cup shortening	½ teaspoon salt
1 cup sugar	1 cup sour milk or buttermilk
1 egg	1 teaspoon soda
2 cups sifted flour	3 tablespoons molasses
½ teaspoon ginger	1 cup blueberries
1 teaspoon cinnamon	3 tablespoons sugar

Cream the shortening and sugar. Add the egg and mix well. Mix and sift together the flour, ginger, cinnamon, and salt, and add to the creamed mixture alternately with the sour milk in which the soda has been dissolved. Add the molasses. Add the blueberries and pour the batter into a greased and floured pan 9 x 9 inches in size. Sprinkle the 3 tablespoons of sugar over the batter in the pan and bake at 350 degrees for 50 minutes to one hour. The sugar sprinkled over the top makes a sweet crusty topping when the cake is baked. This cake is delicious warm from the oven or cold, and even better when 2 days old.

Blueberry Buckle

A dual-purpose confection—coffee cake or dessert—this too appeared in the above pamphlet, credited to Charlotte. (I wonder who Lill and Charlotte are. Anybody know?)

DOUGH

½ cup shortening	2 cups sifted flour
½ cup sugar	½ teaspoon salt
1 egg, beaten	2½ teaspoons baking powder
½ cup milk	

Cream shortening and sugar. Add beaten egg and mix well. Mix and sift the flour, salt, and baking powder together and add to the creamed mixture alternately with the milk. Spread this dough in an 8-inch square pan.

FILLING

2½ cups blueberries	½ cup flour
½ cup sugar	¼ teaspoon cinnamon
1/3 cup butter	

Spread blueberries on the top of the dough. Mix and sift dry ingredients together, then cut the butter in. Spread this over the top of the blueberries. Bake from 1 to 1¼ hours at 375 degrees. Serve warm as a coffee cake or as a dessert. It may be rewarmed by placing in a paper bag, sprinkling the bag with water, and putting it into a warm oven until it is thoroughly heated.

Blueberry Pudding

1 quart fresh blueberries	2 cups bread crumbs
¼ cup flour	¾ cup sugar
2 cups hot milk	Butter

Wash berries and drain thoroughly. Sprinkle flour over berries, let stand 30 minutes. Pour milk over crumbs, add sugar and blueberries. Put this mixture into a greased baking dish, dot with butter, and bake 45 minutes in a moderate oven (360 F.). Serve hot with hard sauce.

Blueberry Sauce

1/3 cup granulated sugar	1 scant cup hot water
1½ tablespoons flour	1 cup blueberries
¼ teaspoon salt	2 teaspoons butter
1 tablespoon lemon juice	2 tablespoons rum

Mix sugar, flour, and salt in saucepan. Add gradually the lemon juice and water. Stir until sauce is smooth and begins to thicken. Add blueberries and continue to cook, stirring constantly until mixture is thick. Remove from heat and beat in butter and rum. Serve hot or warm over ice cream or cake.

Banana Nut Bread

Some years ago Marion Harris introduced us to her banana nut bread, and we have enjoyed it many, many times since. As a matter of fact, we generally have a loaf or two in the freezer, just in case.

1¾ cups sifted flour	1/3 cup shortening
½ teaspoon salt	2/3 cup sugar
2 teaspoons baking powder	1 cup mashed bananas
¼ teaspoon baking soda	2 eggs, well beaten
Chopped	

Sift together flour, salt, baking powder, and baking soda. Beat in the shortening. In a separate dish, add the sugar gradually to the bananas and beat until light and fluffy. Put in the eggs and continue to beat. Add flour mixture alternately with chopped nuts to the banana mixture. Stir and turn into a well-greased pan. Bake in a moderate oven (350 degrees) about 1 hour.

Shredded Wheat Bread

Another delicious bread by Marion Harris:

2 cups boiling water	2 shredded wheat biscuits
2 tablespoons shortening	1 dry yeast cake
2 teaspoons salt	¼ cup warm water
1/3 cup molasses	5 cups flour (about)

Measure the water, shortening, salt, and molasses into a mixing bowl. Crumble the shredded wheat into this. Dissolve the yeast cake in the warm water and add to the above, followed by the flour. Turn out on a floured board and knead for 8 minutes. Grease the mixing bowl, then return bread to rise for about 2 hours. Pound it down, then let it rise again for 1 hour. Turn it out on board and let it relax for 10 minutes. Bake in a 400-degree oven for 45 to 50 minutes.

This makes 2 good-sized loaves

Maine Hot Biscuits

They're made this way on Bailey Island by Florence Leeman.

2 cups flour	1 teaspoon salt
3 teaspoons baking powder	3 tablespoons shortening
	½ cup water

Sift the flour, baking powder, and salt together. Add the shortening, mixing well with a fork. Add the water and mix. Roll out on a floured bread board. Cut with a round cutter and place on a well-greased pan. Brush the biscuits with butter before baking to make them tan and moist. Bake at 450 to 500 degrees until tanned on top.

Corn Meal Muffins or Bread

An old, old Island recipe. Actually there hasn't been any significant change in making them since the old days. Of course, there are mixes available now, but somehow they never seem to taste the same.

1½ cups flour	2 eggs
2/3 cup corn meal	4 tablespoons sugar
3 teaspoons baking powder	½ cup shortening, melted
½ teaspoon salt	2/3 cup milk

Sift together the flour, corn meal, baking powder, and salt. Add the eggs, sugar, melted shortening, and milk and mix well. Put in a greased muffin pan or baking dish.

Makes 12 muffins or 1 good-sized pan of bread

Mrs. Winchell's Soft Johnny Cake

Tom Winchell, an old and good friend, remembered eating this old-fashioned Johnny Cake nearly every morning when he was a child. It was devised by his mother in Brunswick, Maine, around 1880.

1½ cups corn meal	¾ cup sugar
1 teaspoon salt	2 tablespoons milk

Stir meal, salt, and sugar into a small quantity of cold water until smooth. Cook over medium heat, adding hot water until it is the consistency of thick cereal.

Pour into a shallow, buttered pan, spreading it smooth, and spread the milk on top. When placing the pan in a hot oven the mixture should be about ¾ inch thick. Bake until brown.

Mrs. Winchell served it on plates, spreading it quite thin, and putting over it very generous quantities of butter. It was eaten with a fork or a spoon.

Rolled Oats Bread

This is a specialty of Vera Sylvester (Bill Jr.'s wife), who cooks with the best of them here and in addition works with Margaret Richardson in confecting the finest chocolate candy you've ever put into your mouth. (See page 119.)

1¾ cups rolled oats	½ cup molasses
1 tablespoon salt	1 cup scalded milk
2½ cups boiling water	1 yeast cake
¼ cup shortening	½ cup warm milk

9 cups flour

Combine the oats, salt, boiling water, shortening, molasses and scalded milk. Let stand until cool. Add the yeast cake dissolved in the warm milk. Now add the flour. Knead until smooth and let rise to double in bulk. Shape into loaves and let it rise for another hour. Bake in a 400-degree oven for 45 minutes.

Makes 2 loaves

My Father's Popovers

My father liked to cook breakfast. I never knew him to cook anything else except an occasional steak over charcoal. And once in a while he did dunk the lobsters in the boiling water. Breakfast—that was his meal. And that's how he came to make popovers. They were the only hot bread he ever made, but he became expert at it.

Originally, he had to contend with a wood fire. That's all there was in our early days at the cottage. He mastered it all right and never to my knowledge turned out a bad batch. Later there was a coal fire, and still later oil. These more or less modern cooking fires didn't impress him, though they were easier to work with.

1 cup flour, sifted	2 eggs
½ teaspoon salt	1 cup milk

There's nothing particularly special or different about this recipe. Popovers are popovers. Yet somehow his seemed bigger and better, popped to perfection and crisp on the outside.

First he resifted the flour with the salt. Then he lightly beat the eggs and added the milk, and mixed this with the dry ingredients. His batter was always thin and runny. He used iron gem or muffin pans and heated them until they were good and hot, then buttered them well. The batter was poured in to the halfway mark and baked in a hot oven for 20 minutes, then at decreased heat for another 20 to 30 minutes. Today's heats would be 450 degrees then 375 degrees.

Naturally they were served piping hot. There was no delay by my sister and me when Dad called us for breakfast. Usually we were waiting for him at the table.

Oh yes, this recipe will make a dozen beautiful popovers

Steamed Brown Bread

Grandmother Willan always had brown bread to go with her Saturday night baked beans. It was steamed in the oven for the last 4 hours that the beans were baking. She used quart size lard pails. Later there were 3-pound shortening cans.

4 cups white corn meal	1 teaspoon baking powder,
2 cups flour	dissolved in sour milk
¼ teaspoon salt	1 cup molasses
4 cups sour milk	

Sift the meal, flour, and salt together. Add the baking powder, molasses, and sour milk and mix well. Steam in a well-greased covered can for 4 hours. Grandmother used an iron kettle half full of water in the oven and put the can in it. It can be done on the top of the stove, if you prefer.

Four Kinds of Muffins

I like the variations you can effect with this basic recipe. (See below.) Thanks, Alwilda Stackpole!

2 cups flour	2 tablespoons sugar
½ teaspoon salt	1 egg
4 teaspoons baking powder	1 cup milk
3 tablespoons melted fat	

Stir the dry ingredients together in a bowl. Beat the egg and add the milk and melted fat, turning them immediately into the dry ingredients; and stir until just dampened.

Fill greased muffin pans half full and bake in a hot oven, 425 degrees, for about 20 minutes.

Now the variations: for graham muffins replace half the flour with graham flour; for corn muffins replace one third the flour with corn meal; and for bran muffins replace one third the flour with bran.

Four recipes in one! That's what I call efficiency.

Butter 'n' Egg Yeast Bread

Out of a local Harpswell cookbook, this is a bread you'll really like, and not too hard to make.

2 cakes yeast	2 teaspoons salt
½ cup lukewarm water	6¼-7 cups sifted flour
1½ cups scalded milk	¼ cup soft butter
¼ cup sugar	2 eggs

Mix the yeast in warm water. Set aside. Pour the milk over the sugar and salt in a bowl. Stir until dissolved and slightly cool. Add half of the flour and beat until smooth. Beat in the butter, eggs, and the yeast mixture. Add the remaining flour and mix to a soft dough. Turn out on a lightly floured board. Knead 5 to 10 minutes, or until dough becomes smooth and satiny. Place in a greased bowl, grease the top of the dough, and cover with wax paper. Let rise until double in bulk (1 to 1½ hours). Roll out on a board. Shape into loaves and bake 30 to 35 minutes at 425 degrees.

Makes 2 loaves

Molasses Gunjee

I came across this one day at Skillings Boat Yard where Lin Bibber, just about the finest boatbuilder in these parts, was taking time out for lunch. He had finished his sandwiches and was eating what looked to me like gingerbread. "That's gunjee," he said. "My mother used to make it for me when I was a young one. Here, have a piece." It was a soft gingerbread, moist and delicious. Lin didn't know how it got its name. I'm only guessing, so don't hold me to this: it could be a child's way of saying ginger. Do you think so?

1 cup molasses	1 teaspoon ginger
½ cup sugar	1 teaspoon salt
¼ cup shortening, melted	2 cups flour (scant)
1 egg	1 heaping teaspoon soda
1 cup boiling water	

Mix first six ingredients together until well blended. Add the flour. Dissolve the soda in the boiling water, and fold into the batter until well mixed. The batter will be quite thin.

Pour into a greased and floured cake pan. It makes quite a big cake, so be sure your pan is a good size, about 8½ inches square by 2 inches deep. Bake in a moderate oven (350 degrees) for 25 to 30 minutes.

Old-Fashioned Gingerbread

Gingerbread was part and parcel of staying with Grandmother Willan. She always had some in her bakery larder. While it was best piping hot with whipped cream slathered over it, I liked it cold almost as well, particularly when she gave me a bottle of homemade root beer to wash it down.

½ cup butter	2½ cups sifted flour
½ cup sugar	1½ teaspoons baking soda
1 egg, beaten	1 teaspoon cloves
1 cup molasses	1 teaspoon ginger
½ teaspoon salt	1 cup boiling water

First she creamed the butter and sugar, then added the beaten egg and molasses. Now came the dry ingredients and the hot water, the whole mixture to be beaten until smooth. Put into a square or rectangle baking pan or dish, it was baked in a 350 degree oven for about 30 minutes.

Doughnuts

There is a story that it was a Maine man who discovered that cutting a hole in a piece of dough made a better doughnut. Then, of course, he fried the little round pieces and found out they were actually the best part! So that's how-come the holes in doughnuts. Or is it? Here's the easiest way to make plain doughnuts:

2 eggs	1 cup sour milk
1 cup sugar	½ teaspoon salt
4 tablespoons butter, melted	1 teaspoon nutmeg
1 teaspoon soda	3 cups flour (about)

Beat the eggs well and add the sugar and melted butter. Dissolve the soda in the milk and add. Sift the dry ingredients and add, using enough flour to make the dough soft enough to handle. Roll out and cut with a doughnut cutter. Fry in deep hot fat.

Molasses Doughnuts

These call for the same materials as above, except you use half as much sugar (½ cup) and put in 1 cup molasses and 1 teaspoon of ginger. Use the same procedure for putting them together.

Potato Doughnuts

The only acknowledgment I can make of this recipe is to the Maine Department of Economic Development. I found it, hand written, in a file of potato recipes and publicity, the result of an advertising and public relations campaign circa 1938.

4 medium-sized potatoes	½ teaspoon soda
1 tablespoon butter	2 teaspoons baking powder
1 cup sugar	½ teaspoon salt
½ cup sour milk	1 pinch nutmeg
2 eggs, well beaten	Flour sufficient to roll

Peel and boil potatoes until soft; mash them, add butter, and beat until creamy. When cool, add the sugar, sour milk, eggs, soda, baking powder, salt, and nutmeg. Mix enough flour in so it will roll. Fry in deep, hot fat. As the unknown recipe maker said, they're "tender and tasty, and they keep fresh."

Pumpkin Pie

The secret of a really good pumpkin pie is in the preparation of the pumpkin meat. Ethel Doughty in "Maine-ly Recipes," published by the Harpswell P. T. A., cooks it very slowly until it has lost most of its moisture and has taken on a rich, golden brown color.

2 cups cooked, strained pumpkin	¼ teaspoon cloves
	½ teaspoon mace
2 teaspoons melted butter	½ teaspoon ginger
½ teaspoon salt	1 cup milk
1 cup sugar	½ cup cream
½ teaspoon cinnamon	2 eggs, well beaten

Make pastry for a large undercrust. Add to the pumpkin the butter, salt, sugar, spices, milk, cream and eggs. Pour into the pastry-lined pie plate, put into a 450-degree oven for 10 minutes, then reduce the heat to 350 degrees for 30 minutes. Bake until the filling is firm.

Carrot Pie

2 cups strained carrot pulp	2 teaspoons cinnamon
1¼ cups sugar	¼ teaspoon salt
2 teaspoons flour	½ teaspoon ginger
2 eggs	2 cups scalded milk

Beat first 7 ingredients thoroughly, then add the scalded milk. Pour into a pastry-lined pie plate and bake in a 400-degree oven for 15 minutes. Reduce heat to 350 degrees and bake another 45 minutes. Test as for squash or pumpkin pie. This makes a large pie according to Susie Houghton, whose recipe it is.

Duly Apple Dumplings

A favorite here for many generations, this is a dessert that glorifies good Maine apples—and where the name "Duly" came from, I don't know.

2 cups flour	2/3 cup milk
2 teaspoons baking powder	6 apples, sliced thin
1 teaspoon salt	½ cup brown sugar
½ cup shortening	½ teaspoon cinnamon
½ teaspoon nutmeg	

Make a dough and roll it out to ¼-inch thickness in a rectangle about 10 by 16 inches. Cover with the sliced apples and sprinkle with the brown sugar and spices.

Roll up carefully and cut into 1-inch slices. Spread the slices in a large baking pan. Then make a sauce:

LEMON SYRUP

1 cup sugar	¼ teaspoon cinnamon
2 cups water	2 lemons—juice and grated
4 tablespoons butter	rind of one, and very
Pinch of ground cloves	thin slices of the other

Combine these ingredients and cook slowly until syrupy. When ready, spoon the syrup carefully over the top of the slices until you use it all. Then bake in a 400-degree oven for 25 to 30 minutes, or until brown and done.

Aunt Hat's Sponge Cake

Mrs. David Cunningham of Freeport says "I found this

recipe, yellowed with age, in an old box of my mother's recipes. There was more hand beating involved than most of us would want today. Aunt Hat was my great-aunt.

"3 eggs—beat 2 minutes; put in 1½ cups of sugar—beat 5 minutes; 1 cup of flour, 1 even teaspoon of cream of tartar—add them to above and beat 2 minutes; next ½ cup of cold water with ½ teaspoon of soda—beat 2 minutes; fold in 1 cup of flour and ½ teaspoon of lemon extract.

"Beat a little longer and start in a rather slow oven. Increase heat a little and bake about 75 minutes."

Should I say this cake is the "beatinest," or would you rather I didn't?

Mr. Bean's Camp Dessert

The sheer simplicity of this shouldn't fool you. It is delicious.

Mix ½ cup of powdered sugar and 1 cup of butter. Add 2 cups of sifted flour. Roll this quite thin, cut in squares, and bake.

Thus L. L. Bean's instructions. And he adds "Try this recipe at home." I have.

New Meadows Inn Cookies

If you've been in this part of Maine you have no doubt heard of New Meadows Inn where the shore dinner is a classic. This, of course, is the new New Meadows Inn on the Bath Road, where the New Meadows River flows under it. The old Inn which burned down many, many years ago was well off the road, and one of the Casco Bay steamers used to bring a daily boatload from Portland and the islands for a noontime feast. If I recall correctly, when I was a young boy the dinner cost 75 cents. It consisted of steamed clams, lobster stew, fried clams, and a whole boiled lobster. (You could have seconds on the stew!) Dessert was simple—doughnuts, or cookies like these:

½ cup butter	½ teaspoon soda
1 cup sugar	½ teaspoon salt
1 egg	½ teaspoon nutmeg
2½ cups flour	½ teaspoon mace
1 teaspoon cream of tartar	1/3 cup milk

Cream the butter, add the sugar, and beat until light and fluffy. Add the egg. Sift the dry ingredients together, then add alternately with milk to the creamed butter mixture. Chill overnight. Then roll out very thin, cut out with cookie cutter, and bake at 375 degrees until light brown.

Makes 10 dozen cookies

Twiddie's Molasses Cookies

The origin of these cookies is not known to Ruth Bibber, Lin's wife. They've been made in the family for at least three generations, but no one remembers "Twiddie." When baked they are almost ⅜ of an inch thick and fairly soft, which is the way molasses cookies ought to be.

Cream 1 cup of shortening with 1 cup of sugar. Add 2 eggs and a cup of molasses. Sift together 3½ cups of flour, 2 teaspoons of soda, 1 teaspoon of salt, 1 teaspoon of ginger, and 1 teaspoon of cinnamon. Add alternately with ½ cup of cold water. Drop large spoonfuls on a cookie sheet and bake in a moderate oven.

Eggless Chocolate Cake

Pru Boyce has three growing boys and a hungry husband. Like an army they move on their stomachs, or so it seems. Judging by their looks, Pru does all right by them. Her chocolate cake helps.

1 2/3 cups flour	1 teaspoon salt
1 cup sugar	1 cup sour milk
¾ cup cocoa	½ cup melted butter
1 teaspoon baking soda	1 teaspoon vanilla

Sift the dry ingredients together. Add the milk, butter, and vanilla. Stir until smooth. Bake in a 350-degree oven in a greased 8 x 8 x 2-inch pan. Or if you prefer, bake it in layers, and put it together with frosting.

Kenneth Roberts's Chocolate Custards

This fine recipe from "Trending into Maine," like the other two Roberts specials published herein, appeared in "The World's Best Recipes," by Marvin Small. We're privileged to use it.

3 heaping tablespoons of cornstarch dissolved in ½ cup of milk	2 tablespoons of water 1 square of cooking chocolate
2½ cups of milk 5 heaping tablespoons of sugar	½ teaspoon vanilla extract Cream

The following instructions are as they were originally written by Mr. Roberts. I'll omit the quotes.

1. The first step in making chocolate custards is to buy two or three dozen glass goblets—the sort shaped like large egg cups.

2. Three heaping tablespoons of cornstarch are dissolved in half a cup of milk.

3. Two-and-one-half cups of milk are heated in a double boiler. Into a saucepan are put five heaping tablespoons of sugar, two tablespoons of water, one square of cooking chocolate.

4. This is dissolved over boiling water, then placed on the fire, boiled for two minutes, and added to the hot milk.

5. When the mixture has the appearance of chocolate milk instead of plain milk, the half cup of milk and cornstarch is poured in. It is stirred until slightly thickened, when a half teaspoon of vanilla extract is added.

6. It is then poured into the goblets, and the latter, when

cool, are placed in the icebox. Before serving, cream is added to the surface with a gentle hand, so not to break the delicate scum.

Makes 6 servings

Butterscotch Bread Pudding

With or without the butterscotch touch, a bread pudding is always a good dessert. Economical, too.

1 cup brown sugar	3 eggs
4 slices buttered bread,	2 cups milk
cubed	1 teaspoon vanilla
½ teaspoon salt	

Put the brown sugar in a double boiler. Add the bread. Beat the eggs and add the milk, vanilla, and salt. Pour over the bread. Cook over boiling water for 1 hour. Do not stir.

Hannah Munsey's Brown Betty

2 cups stale bread crumbs	½ cup sugar
¼ cup butter, melted	½ teaspoon cinnamon
3 cups sliced apples	2 tablespoons water
2 tablespoons lemon juice	

Mix the crumbs with the melted butter. Arrange alternate layers of apples and bread crumbs in a baking dish, sprinkling each layer with sugar and cinnamon. Pour water and lemon juice over last layer, and cover. Bake in a moderate oven, removing cover the last 15 minutes. Brown sugar or molasses and white sugar may be used instead of the ½ cup of sugar. Vanilla ice cream is a fine topping.

Strawberry Cobbler

If you could be here when the wild strawberries are ripe, you would have a dessert of such perfection that it would merit a place among the best in the world. With regular berries or even frozen ones it is still a great confection.

First make a fruit sauce: Put a basket of strawberries (or a large package of frozen berries that have been thawed) into a saucepan. Combine and blend ½ cup of sugar and two teaspoons of cornstarch, then add ¾ cup of water. Mix and add to the strawberries. Heat to boiling point, stirring constantly. Pour into casserole.

Now make the dumplings: sift together 1 cup of flour, ½ teaspoon of salt, 1½ teaspoons of baking powder, ¼ cup of sugar. Add 3 tablespoons of shortening, and cut in. Then add ½ cup of milk. Mix and drop by small spoonfuls on the hot sauce. Sprinkle with sugar. Bake at 400 degrees for about 30 minutes. Serve with whipped cream.

I have an idea this would be equally good with raspberries or blackberries. Try it next summer and see.

Harpswell Upside-Down Pudding

One thing I like about this dessert: it's complete with sauce when baked.

1 cup flour	½ cup milk
2 tablespoons baking powder	2 teaspoons melted butter
¼ teaspoon salt	1 cup nut meats
¾ cup sugar	1 cup brown sugar
1½ tablespoons cocoa	4 tablespoons cocoa
1¾ cups hot water	

Sift the first five ingredients together and add the milk and melted butter. Blend in the nuts. Pour into a well-greased baking dish.

Combine the brown sugar with the 4 tablespoons of cocoa and sprinkle this over the batter. Pour the hot water over all and bake 45 minutes at 350 degrees.

Ruth Coffin's Indian Pudding

In her own chapter in her husband's "Mainstays of

Maine," Ruth Coffin wrote engagingly about desserts. And of this one she said:

Of all my desserts, this is my jewel: Indian Pudding. (It is old, it came from the Indians really.) It should cook for hours if possible, at 200 degrees. The stunt is to bake it Saturday with the beans. It can, of course, be baked by rule for two and a half hours. But six or eight hours at the lower temperature is the ideal. Scald 3 cups of milk and stir into it 3 tablespoons of corn meal. Add one third of a cup of molasses, and cook until it thickens, stirring constantly. Remove from the fire, add one half of a cup of sugar, one beaten egg, butter the size of a walnut, one fourth of a teaspoon of salt, one half teaspoon of ginger, and one half teaspoon of cinnamon. Pour into a buttered baking dish and place in a 300 degree oven. After a half hour, pour over it one cup of milk, put it back, leave it with the beans. Let it mature with them. This dessert should be served piping hot, with vanilla ice cream . . .

It is the best dessert in Christendom. It is as American as maple sugar, popcorn, and barefooted boys. It tastes of all three. It is the silk of the corn and the honey of America . . .

Thus spake Ruth Coffin! And, believe me, she knew whereof she spake.

To please the sweet and the sour Maine tooth
There are many concoctions—in sooth
　　The jams and the candies
　　And pickles are dandies,
The jellies and the relishes couth.

VIII

THE SWEET AND SOUR MAINE TOOTH

It may seem incongruous, this grouping together of the sweets and the sours, the jellies and jams and candies, the pickles and relishes and ketchup. But there is some logic behind it: most of them are for future use, canned or preserved and stored away to enhance meals to come. Even candy belongs here, for it too is an added attraction, not a main part of a meal.

I don't know why I worry about it. Doing it this way makes for a better chapter heading, so I'll stand on that specious reasoning.

One thing is sure: these are good recipes, as tried and true as any in the book and eminently worth the effort it takes to prepare and bring into being the finished products.

FOR THE SWEET TOOTH

There are plenty of raw materials in the gardens and fields of Maine to provide a good selection of jams and jellies. Home-made candies are still popular despite the variety of boughten confections available. Speaking of the latter, there are the Orr's Island Candies, than which there are no finer. (See page 119). All in all the Maine sweet tooth is well taken care of.

Strawberry or Raspberry Jam

As always, freshly picked berries are best, particularly the wild ones that are to be found in so many places around here. If you can't pick them yourself, get them at a roadside stand: they were picked the day before.

4 cups berries	1 tablespoon vinegar
3 cups sugar	

Crush the berries, add the vinegar, and bring to a rolling boil for

113

1 minute. Add the sugar and boil for 20 minutes more. Put into scalded jars. This jam will keep its flavor and color indefinitely.
Note: Jams without the addition of fruit pectin are softer and runnier. You may prefer them that way.

Blackberry Jam

Crush completely 2 quarts of blackberries. Sieve the pulp to remove most of the seeds. This should yield 4 cups of juice. Measure it into a large saucepan. Add 7 cups of sugar and mix well. Bring to a full rolling boil over high heat and boil for 1 minute, stirring constantly. Remove from heat and stir in ½ bottle of fruit pectin (Certo). Skim off foam with metal spoon. Continue to stir and skim for 5 minutes to cool slightly and prevent floating fruit. Ladle into jelly glasses and cover immediately with ⅛ inch of hot paraffin.

Makes about 10 medium-size glasses

Blackberry and Apple Jelly

Sadie Nason made me a batch of this last summer of blackberries picked from the wild patch back of the house and apples from our one remaining tree. There's more to making it than a jam but the results are beautiful.

Sadie uses 4 quarts of apples to 2 quarts of blackberries. Cup up the apples—skins, cores, seeds and all—and combine them with the berries in a good-size kettle with enough water to cover. Boil at least 20 minutes.

Drip the mixture through a cheesecloth bag overnight. In the morning measure the juice and use 1 cup of sugar for each cup of juice. Boil for about 20 minutes—the time it takes to jell. Test it: when it jells dropping off the spoon, it's ready to be ladled into sterilized jelly glasses, to be sealed immediately with ⅛ inch of hot paraffin.

There's no need to add pectin to this recipe: the apples make it jell.

Blueberry Jam

Crush 1½ quarts of ripe berries. You should have 4½ cups to measure into a large kettle. Put in 2 tablespoons of lemon juice. Add 7 cups of sugar and mix. Bring to full rolling boil over high heat for 1 minute, stirring constantly. Remove from heat and pour in a bottle of fruit pectin (Certo). Skim off foam then stir and skim for another 5 minutes to cool a bit. Ladle into glasses and cover with hot paraffin.

Makes about 12 medium glasses

Rhubarb Jam

Another item from "Maine-ly Recipes," the Harpswell P. T. A. compendium by the local ladies.

5 cups rhubarb, chopped fine	2 cups sugar
1 cup sugar	1 package jello (strawberry or pineapple)

Let the rhubarb and 1 cup of sugar stand overnight. In the morning put in the other 2 cups of sugar and cook as for a sauce. When it's ready, add the package of jello, mix well, place in jars and seal with hot paraffin.

Makes 6-8 jars

Old-Fashioned Green Tomato Preserves

This is an old Orr's Island recipe, descending from Mrs. Elsie McGowan's grandmother, and as she puts it, it's "real nice and tasty."

¾ pound white sugar	Preserved ginger
1 lemon, sliced	1 pound green tomatoes

Melt the sugar to a syrup with a little water, the lemon, and a little preserved ginger.

Wash the tomatoes and slice or cut into dices. Cook them in slightly salted water for a few minutes. Take them out carefully so they don't break up and add them to the syrup. Cook until amber colored and quite thick. This recipe makes only a small amount. You can multiply it and make enough to fill a few mason jars.

Rose Hip Jam

The way the wild roses grow here there seem to be enough rose hips in the fall of the year to make a reasonably sized commercial enterprise out of making this vitamin D-rich jam. For a moderate amount:

2 cups of hips (before seeding)	1 cup water
1½ cups sugar	2 tablespoons lemon juice

Take the seeds out of the berries and you'll have about 1½ cups left. Boil the sugar and water for 4 minutes. Add the hips and the lemon juice, cover and boil for 15 minutes. Uncover and boil 5 minutes. By this time the berries will be clear and transparent and the syrup thick. Pour into hot, sterilized jars and seal. In case the hips are unusually ripe (before the frost has touched them) add more lemon juice.

Trudy's Apple Sauce

There are other ways of making apple sauce, but for our taste and that of our friends, my wife's is best. I think it's because the entire apple—skin, core, seeds, and all—goes into it. It's the epitome of simplicity: the only real work involved is sieving it when it's done.

First, make a syrup of equal parts sugar and water seasoned with a little grated lemon rind. (If you have 3 pounds of apples, use a cup each of water and sugar.) While the syrup is simmering, cut the apples into quarters. When they are ready add them to the syrup and cook at medium heat until the apples are mushy. Strain through a sieve, let it cool, and refrigerate it until you're ready to use it.

We generally make sizable quantities and freeze quart containers of it.

Mr. Bean's Camp Pancake Syrup

If you don't have any maple syrup with you, this, according to L. L. Bean, is what you can do:

"Add ½ cup of water to 1 cup of brown sugar. Boil for 15 or 20 minutes, remove from stove and cool. When cool, place in bottle or jar for future use.

"If maple sugar is available, take along a few cakes. Add 50 per cent water and boil for about 15 minutes."

There's no truly adequate substitute for pure maple syrup itself but in a pinch either of the above will do.

Brown Sugar Two-Tone Fudge

Phyllis Blackwell, besides being the Harpswell tax collector, is one of our better cooks. This is her candy.

LIGHT MIXTURE:	DARK MIXTURE:
2 cups brown sugar	2 cups brown sugar
1 cup milk	1 cup milk
Butter, size of walnut	4 tablespoons cocoa
1 teaspoon vanilla	Butter, size of walnut
	1 teaspoon vanilla

Make the light mixture first. Cook the brown sugar, milk, and butter until it forms a soft ball. Add the vanilla. Beat and pour into an 8-inch square pan. Let it cool while making the dark mixture.

Cook the brown sugar, milk, cocoa, and butter the same as for the light mixture. Add the vanilla. Pour on top of first batch and let stand until set. Cut into squares. Walnuts may be added to both mixtures.

Aunt Lesley's Penuche

It was a rare treat, and usually on a rainy day, when my Aunt Lesley made a pan of penuche for us. In my young mind it was the most wonderful candy ever. Rich and sweet, it had a short life.

1 package light brown sugar	½ cup nut meats
1½ cups white sugar	¼ stick butter
1 cup milk	1 teaspoon vanilla

Cook first three ingredients until a soft ball forms in water, then add the nut meats, butter, and vanilla. Beat until it starts to thicken, then pour into a pan, let it cool and set, and cut into squares.

Waiting for it to cool tried my patience to the limit.

Cocoanut Potato Candy

By Charlotte Stevens in the Orr's Island Treasure of Personal Recipes.

Boil 1 small Maine potato, peel, and mash fine. Add 1 tablespoon butter, 1 package confectioner's sugar, 1 cup cocoanut and 1 teaspoon of vanilla. Beat all together. Put in ungreased pan. Then pour 1 square of melted chocolate over it. Cut into squares.

Ash Cove Molasses Taffy Pull

This is the way it was before paved roads, radios, indoor plumbing, and an automobile in every yard. We made our own fun at the Ash Cove cottage and this was part of it.

The molasses candy was easy to make, using a cup of molasses, a cup of sugar, and a tablespoon of butter. This was stirred until the sugar dissolved, then cooked over medium heat until a little of the mixture dropped into cold water formed hard threads. We stirred it as it cooled and finally poured it into a greased candy sheet, folding the edges toward the center as they cooled off. This was done so the edges wouldn't harden before the center was ready to pull. (Taffy that has not cooled will stick to the pan.)

When it's cool enough to handle make it into a big ball and pull with buttered fingers until it's light in color. It should be pulled finally into a long rope about ½ inch wide and then cut into 1 inch pieces. Wrap it in wax paper or put on a buttered plate in a cold place—if it lasts that long.

ORR'S ISLAND CANDIES COME IN 26 DELICIOUS FLAVORS

Orr's Island Candies belong in this book. They are made here and sold here. I can give you no recipes for making them. Even if I could you would never be able to equal the results that Margaret Richardson achieves in her kitchen overlooking the back shore and the ledge-studded water that stretches to infinity. The view from her windows alone is enough to warrant a visit. And the candies? Once in her kitchen sampling her chocolates, you will become a lifelong addict. I don't care what candy you have eaten before: this is the greatest!

Margaret Richardson has been making candy for over thirty years. It all started quite modestly when she began dipping chocolates for her family and friends. In subsequent years she has developed her art and production. Made of top ingredients, in comparatively small quantities, each step in the making is carefully controlled. Margaret is a true artist whose pride in her work permits no compromise, no short cuts, no batch offered for sale unless it meets her exacting standards.

You choose what you want from 26 kinds of chocolates: peppermints, caramels, nougats, butter crunch, creams, four kinds of fudge, peanut brittle, molasses chips—come see for yourself. It's all there in front of you, always fresh, and packed as you want it.

Most of the candies are sold locally. As a matter of fact, Margaret and her two assistants are kept busy during the summer season keeping up with the demand of gift shops and stores just around here.

Don't miss this experience when you're in the neighborhood. Margaret will be glad to see you and show you how it's done.

FOR THE SOUR TOOTH

Pickles and other condiments have always been part of the daily fare in Maine, adding zest to meals and in-between snacks, of which there are many in child-filled households particularly. Among the old recipes are the few I have selected, which should fill the bill for most occasions.

Bread and Butter Pickles

I would like to present every purchaser of this book with a jar of the bread and butter pickles we made here last fall. But that's a little visionary, I guess. So make some yourself from this recipe, and you'll have a little over 6 pints of the best bread and butter pickles you ever ate.

You will need 4 quarts of cucumbers, sliced thin, and 3 medium onions, diced. Put them in a pan and cover with ½ cup of salt· and about a cup of water. Then lay ice cubes on top, cover, and let stand overnight. Next morning drain and rinse well with fresh cold water.

In a pan large enough to accommodate the cucumbers and onions, boil the following together for 3 minutes:

4 cups white vinegar	¼ teaspoon ground cloves
1 cup water	2 tablespoons mustard seed
3 cups white sugar	1 teaspoon celery seed
2 cups brown sugar	1 teaspoon turmeric

Add the cucumbers, etc., and simmer for 15 or 20 minutes, or until the cucumbers become transparent. Pack in hot sterilized jars and seal.

You can put in a couple of diced green peppers, if you like. We prefer them without this addition.

Makes 6-7 pints

Ruth Bibber's 9 Day Pickles

These take 9 days from start to finish—not 9 days of steady work, heaven forbid, but a little work every three days until they're jarred. They are a delightful combination of sweet and sour, and they'll keep well if you want them to.

For 3 days, soak 7 pounds of cucumbers (whole and without removing stems, etc.) in salt water that will float an egg. On the 4th day cut off stems and split them lengthwise into convenient slices. Soak them in fresh water for 3 more days.

On the 7th day place them in a weak solution of vinegar and water and 1 teaspoon of powdered alum. Heat 1½ hours. **Do not boil.** Drain. Make a syrup of 6 cups of sugar and 3 pints of vinegar. Let this come to a boil. Add ½ dozen sticks of cinnamon and ½ dozen whole cloves and add drained pickles. Heat this each day, without boiling, for 3 days. Seal hot on the 9th day.

Lin Bibber, Ruth's husband, had a surplus of cucumbers this fall and gave me more than enough to make these and the bread and butter pickles. As the saying goes " they are some good!"

Maine-ly Sweet Pickles

Maybe pickle making runs in the Bibber family. These are by Beverly Bibber in the Harpswell cookbook "Maine-ly Recipes."

8 quarts cucumbers	10 cups sugar
3 sweet red peppers	1 teaspoon turmeric
2 sweet green peppers	1 teaspoon ground cloves
2 cauliflowers	1 teaspoon celery seed
¾ gallon button onions	¼ teaspoon mustard seed
¾ cup salt	2½ quarts vinegar

Cut up the cucumbers and peppers, break up the cauliflowers into small pieces, use the onions whole, and mix salt through the mixture. Place in a large kettle and weight the lid. Let stand for 3 hours. Drain and add the remaining ingredients. Put over low heat and heat well but do not boil. Seal in hot sterilized jars.

Mustard Pickles

This is not from a Bibber household, but it's a very successful process.

1 quart onions, cut up	6 tablespoons dry mustard
1 quart green tomatoes, cut up	1 tablespoon turmeric
2 quarts cucumbers, peeled and cut up	1 cup sugar
	1 cup flour
1 large head of cauliflower, separated into small pieces	2 quarts vinegar

Soak the onions, tomatoes, cucumbers, and cauliflower in a weak brine for 24 hours (1 cup salt to a gallon of water). Then scald them in the brine and drain. Mix the other ingredients in a little vinegar until smooth. Add the rest of the vinegar and strain. Boil it until it is as thick as cream. Finally add the pickle mixture and boil for about 15 minutes. Seal in hot, sterilized jars.

Piccalilli

Another Beverly Bibber special!

1 peck green tomatoes	1½ teaspoons ground cloves
2 cups salt	2½ teaspoons cinnamon
½ peck of onions	8 teaspoons nutmeg
4 medium hot green peppers	8 to 10 cups sugar
5 large sweet red peppers	5 cups pure cider vinegar

This will make a lot, so be sure you have a big enough kettle and enough jars. Grind the tomatoes, cover with 2 cups of salt and let stand overnight. In the morning drain and wash well. Grind the onions and peppers, add sugar and the spices (tied in a cloth bag). Add vinegar. Bring to a boil and boil gently for about 2 hours. Remove the spice bag. Seal piccalilli in hot, sterilized jars.

Pickled Eggs and Red Beets

Boil young beets until tender. Skin and cover with a liquid made as follows: ¼ cup brown sugar, ½ cup vinegar, ½ cup cold water, a small piece of cinnamon, 3 or 4 cloves—all boiled together for 10 minutes. Let the beets stand in the liquid for several days. Remove the beets and put in 2 shelled, whole, hard-cooked eggs and let them pickle for 2 days. Put the beets back in and they are ready to use.

Green Tomato Relish

Several years ago as I walked into Mildred Hillman's store there was the most wonderful aroma coming out of the kitchen in back. "What's cooking?" I asked. "Oh, that's my green tomato relish," she answered. "Want some?" Silly question! And ever since then we've made it ourselves.

Mildred, like so many good cooks, doesn't need precise directions: her taste and the way things look tell her when they are right. This is the way she makes it:

Use twice as many tomatoes as onions (in bulk). Slice them, keeping separate. Boil the onions in 1 pan until soft. Boil the tomatoes in another pan. Don't let them get too soft. Drain both and combine in a kettle and pour in enough vinegar to cook them and add a cup or more of sugar. Cook them over moderate heat about a half hour, tasting to see if that's the way you like them. Then remove from the heat and let sit overnight. Reheat in the morning and seal in pint or quart jars.

Grandmother Roberts's Homemade Tomato Ketchup

In " Trending into Maine " Kenneth wrote:

Such was the passion for my grandmother's ketchup in my own family that we could never get enough of it. We were allowed to have it on beans, fish cakes and hash, since those dishes were acknowledged to be incomplete without it; but when we went so far as to demand it on bread, as we often did, we were peremptorily refused, and had to go down in the cellar to steal it—which we also often did. It had a savory, appetizing tang to it that seemed—and still seems—to me to be inimitable. I became almost a ketchup drunkard; for when I couldn't get it, I yearned for it. Because of that yearning, I begged the recipe from my grandmother when I went away from home; and since that day I have made many and many a batch of her ketchup with excellent results.

The recipe has never been published, and I put it down here for the benefit of those who aren't satisfied with the commercial makeshifts that masquerade under the name of ketchup.

Makes about 1 gallon:

1 peck ripe tomatoes, cooked and strained, or 1 dozen cans of concentrated tomato juice	2 tablespoons mustard
	1 tablespoon powdered cloves
	1 teaspoon black pepper
	¼ teaspoon red pepper
1 pint sharp vinegar	Olive oil
6 tablespoons salt	4 tablespoons allspice

1. With a large spoon rub cooked tomatoes through a sieve into a kettle, to remove seeds and heavy pulp, until you have 1 gallon of liquid. One peck of ripe tomatoes, cooked and strained, makes one gallon. (This operation is greatly simplified by using one dozen cans of concentrated tomato juice.)

2. Put the kettle on the stove and bring the tomato juice almost to a boil.

3. Into a bowl put a pint of sharp vinegar, and in the vinegar dissolve 6 tablespoons of salt, 4 tablespoons of allspice, 2 tablespoons of mustard, 1 tablespoon of powdered cloves, 1 teaspoon of black pepper and ¼ teaspoon of red pepper.

4. Stir the vinegar and spices into the tomato juice, set the kettle over a slow fire and let it simmer until it thickens. The mixture must be constantly stirred, or the spices settle on the bottom and burn. If made from concentrated tomato juice, an hour and a half of simmering is sufficient; but if made from cooked tomatoes, the mixture should be allowed to cook slowly for 3 or 4 hours.

5. When the kettle is removed from the fire, let the mixture stand until cold.

6. Then stir and pour into small-necked bottles. If a half inch of olive oil is poured into each bottle, and the bottle then corked, the ketchup will keep indefinitely in a cool place. It's better if chilled before serving.

Brine For Salt Pork

Chances are you'll never do this, but it goes to show how simple it is and why people had so much salt pork in their cellars.

Use a keg big enough and enough cold water to cover what salt pork you want to make. Add salt until the brine floats a potato. Put the pork in and weight it down to keep it from floating. Leave it alone for a month or more.

SOAP

This seems to me to be a fitting end to "What's Cooking Down in Maine." If you'll pardon me, it sort of cleans it up! It's here for you to use if the spirit or the need arises. Many of the women on the Casco Bay Islands still make soap. Why not you?

5 pounds old fat	¼ cup ammonia
1 cup lye	2 tablespoons sugar
4 cups cold water	4 tablespoons borax
¼ cup kerosene	

Heat the fat until lukewarm, then strain it. Add the rest of the ingredients and mix together until thick. Pour into a small cardboard box lined with tinfoil. Cut into squares before it gets too hard. It's better to keep awhile before using.

HAIL AND FAREWELL

There is a considerable quantity of other Maine recipes, equal in quality and appeal, perhaps, to those I have culled. And there are doubtless a large number of dishes from other sections of the country and the world that would be even better for using Maine materials and products.

But as I said earlier, this book does not pretend to be all-inclusive: it is a sampler. Thus if it whets your appetite and brings you into closer rapport with all Maine cookery, it will have achieved its purpose. And I will have done you a favor.

I hope you will enjoy cooking with "What's Cooking Down in Maine" as much as I have enjoyed writing it (and testing it, too). The Maine way of cooking is sound: it stands up with the best and makes of the simplest ingredients honest, wholesome and flavor-full dishes.

May good Maine food help you to the long, healthful life that is the prime blessing Maine can bestow!

Index

129

130

132